Addie of the Flint Hills

A Prairie Child During the Depression (1915–1935)

Addie of the Flint Hills

A Prairie Child During the Depression (1915–1935)

Adaline Sorace
as told to Deborah Sorace Prutzman

KTAV Publishing House, Inc.

Library of Congress Cataloging-in-Publication Data

Sorace, Adaline, 1915-Addie of the Flint Hill: a prairie child during the depression
(1915-1935)/Adaline Sorace as told to Deborah Sorace Prutzman.
    p. cm.
ISBN 978-1-60280-123-3

1. Sorace, Adaline, 1915–Childhood and youth–Anecdotes. 2. Chase County
(Kan.)–Social life and customs–20th century–Anecdotes.
3. Depressions–1929–Kansas–Chase County–Anecdotes.
4. Chase County (Kan.)–Biography–Anecdotes. 5. Country life–Kansas–Chase
County–Anecdotes. 6. Flint Hills (Kan. and Okla.)–Social life and customs–
20th century–Anecdotes. 7. Flint Hills (Kan. and Okla.)–Biography–Anecdotes. I. Title.

F687.C35S68 2009
978.1'59032092--dc22

2009010593

Published by
KTAV Publishing House, Inc.
930 Newark Avenue, Jersey City, N.J. 07306
www.ktav.com
Email: orders@ktav.com
Phone: 201-963-9524 • Fax: 201-963-0102

Acknowledgements

We wish to express our deep appreciation
for the assistance given by so many, but especially to:

The Kansas State Historical Society, which provides comprehensive resources for those studying the history of Kansas and its people. Substantial guidance was provided to us by Sara Keckeisen and Lisa Keys. In addition, the photographs on pages 18 (top), 50, 82, 85, 86, 87, 90, 96, 101, 105, 112, 170, and 186 are provided courtesy of the Kansas State Historical Society.

Chase County Historical Society Museum and Library, located in Cottonwood Falls, Kansas. Housed in a building that has been entered on the National Register of Historic Places, it is dedicated to preserving the history of this scenic area. We especially appreciate the efforts of the Historical Society's Museum Director, Carla Gallmeister, to find suitable photographs. The fruits of her labor, found on pages 32, 59, 103, 108, and 119, are provided courtesy of the Chase County Historical Society.

The Pioneer Bluffs Foundation, which is located on the historic headquarters of the Rogler Ranch, founded in 1859. Pioneer Bluffs was designated a National Register Historic District in 1992. The photographs found on pages 100 and 106 were provided courtesy of Pioneer Bluffs. Marva Weigelt, Pioneer Bluffs' Project Historian, provided much help and encouragement.

Jane Koger, owner of Homestead Ranch, a working cattle ranch in the heart of Chase County. Jane provided enthusiastic support and the photos found on pages 114 and 164. Jane is a granddaughter of Roy Beedle.

Lloyd Rogler, a grandson of Albert Rogler, read several versions of the manuscript and always asked the right questions.

Terry and Marcella Swanson for sharing family photos and memories, and their enthusiasm. Terry is the son of my beloved sister, Elsie Rene.

Finally, **Darrel Johnson**, a grandson of Mable Beedle, provided the photos on pages 68, 118, 128 and 165 and valuable historic information about the Beedle family. He was there at the beginning and his encouragement never wavered.

Dedicated to my grandchildren,
Sarah, Stephen, Cheryl and Brian,
and my children,
Deborah and James

Introduction

As I was growing up in a suburb of New York City my mother would tell me, from time to time, about her childhood on a farm in the Flint Hills of Kansas. These tales, told before bed or during a pause in our daily activities, always involved short little stories. They usually included an amused mention of her sister Elsie Rene or a tad of family lore followed by the reverential mention of "Great-Aunt Adaline." I listened because sometimes she talked about Indians and pioneers and, back in the 1950s, the Davy Crockett television series was all the rage. Time went by and the stories became but faint memories.

By the summer of 2007 Mom was in her 90s and living close to me when a beloved sister-in-law died. After knowing and loving my Aunt for nearly 60 years, Mom was discouraged and wondered what remaining purpose she had on this earth. I could never remember Mom speaking like that; she was always the optimist looking ahead. Faintly recalling the stories from my childhood, I suggested that Mom write about her life. After all, her grandchildren had never known the land and prairie spirit her family represented. I thought there might be a valuable lesson for the children in all this, and at least they would get to know their history. I was thinking about a timeline filling in key events such as the Civil War and the Kansas Nebraska Act. These would become more meaningful to the kids as they learned what roles their ancestors played, I reasoned.

Little did I know! Mom began to write a story for our times.

The very next day as I came over for a cup of coffee she pre-sented me with 20 handwritten pages. I typed them, and later discussed them with her. Why did this happen? What else did someone say? What was Grandpa really like? Mom's ability to recall the details of her past, dates and all, was astounding. I realized I had never really appreciated her sharp mind before. The details of daily life that she recalled highlighted the distance between the agrarian America into which she was borne and today. I began to see my mother as a young barefoot girl, shaped by the people and times around her. I began to see her tremendous strength and her loving heart, which continued big and full of hope despite all she had lived through.

Then, I realized that Mom's story had relevance today. Her tales of a rise in commodities followed by an increase in borrowing and a bust, began to seem all too close to home. My brother and I watched our investments melt away and began to worry about the future of our children who are starting their adult lives during some very unsettled times. But because I was working on Mom's story, I knew that these events were small when measured against the hardships that Addie and those of her generation had to face. And I realized that even as my mother endured the deprivations of the Great Depression and the Dust Bowl, she knew that her grandparents, early settlers in the Kansas territory, endured equally harsh, even worse conditions, and lived to build a better life. They had an abiding faith in progress, education and community.

This book is an ode to Addie, to her loving, forward-looking spirit, to her willingness to tell the honest truth (even when it does not show her in the best light) and to her belief, which continues today, that we can build a better world.

Deborah Prutzman
New York City, New York
April, 2009

Contents

Addie and Deborah

Timeline

1850–70 Plains Indians exchange land for reservations

1854   Upper half of Indian Territory becomes part of Kansas Territory

1857   Kansas ratifies anti-slavery constitution

1859   Roglers arrive in Kansas; Charles Darwin writes *Origin of Species*

1861   Kansas admitted as state; Abraham Lincoln elected president

1861–65 Civil War

1868   Federal employees get eight-hour workday

1869–76 U.S. Cavalry wars against Plains Indians

1869   Union Pacific meets Central Pacific

1876   Alexander Graham Bell patents telephone

1879   Thomas Alva Edison invents incandescent light

1910   Wheat 80 cents a bushel

1912   Woodrow Wilson elected president

1914   World War I begins, Germany invades Belgium

1915   Addie born; wheat $1.60 a bushel as war drives up prices

1917   United States declares war on Germany; farm prices continue upward, government guarantees grain at $2.00 a bushel

1918   November 11, end of World War I; farm prices fall

1920   Eighteenth Amendment prohibits alcohol; Nineteenth Amendment gives women the vote

1920   Warren G. Harding elected president

1928   Addie and family move to Utah; wheat $1.00 a bushel

1929   Stock market crashes; wheat 75 cents a bushel; 25% of U.S. population still on the farm

1930   Worldwide Depression begins; 1,350 U.S. banks fail

1931   Addie and family move to Beedle Ranch in Kansas; Depression deepens; last significant rain for seven years

1932   Addie and family return to Matfield Green; the "dusters" start; a third of all farms on Plains face foreclosure

1932   Franklin Delano Roosevelt elected president

1933   Roosevelt begins New Deal; closes banks by executive order

1934–39 Dust Bowl ravages American Plains

Addie at 93 Photography by Studio of Christopher Beane

Prologue

Ouch. A sharp pain shot down the length of my left middle finger. I opened my eyes, checked the time. It was 2:00 a.m. Every morning I had the pain at precisely this time. I wondered how the finger knew what time it was.

I turned on the light, grabbed a pain patch from my bedside stand and put it on the throbbing finger. Then turned the light off. Tense, I waited in the dark for the pain to subside. And it did so gradually. I returned to sleep.

Next it was 5:00 a.m. Too early to get up; still, I was wide-awake. I sat on the side of my bed. My head was dizzy, so I waited a few minutes before I stood up. Slowly I tried to walk. The pain in my lower back was really nasty with each step. My feet felt numb. I had to get to the bathroom. I grabbed my walker and started on the way. My knees came to life, aching and paining. I made it to the bathroom without accident.

Then came the massage chair—a gift from my daughter. Carefully, with deliberation, I settled in the chair and started the back massage. My muscles relaxed. As it worked away I felt better.

It was my ninety-second birthday.

I looked around the room and thought how different things were from the day I was born. August 8, 1915. There was no TV, no radio, no electric light, no air-conditioning, no central heating, and no massage chair. Virtually nothing I saw in the early morning light existed on the day I was born.

I let my mind drift. I recalled reading once about a man who in-sisted that he remembered how it was in his mother's womb. My memory is not that good. But I do remember my parents telling me about my birth, on a humble farm in the Kansas Flint Hills. We were close to nature there–the sky, the rain and the earth were all elements in our very survival.

I looked outside my window: bricks and the top of the Empire State building with its tower of lights. I wondered at the creativity that changed a quiet farming island into a world of bricks, cement and steel; miles of roads and tunnels and people of every color. All talking on their cell phones, all honking their car horns, all moving. Yes, I am in New York City.

Dear Mother and Dad, you never dreamed what my life would be like! Or what the world would be like 90 years later!

It has been a long trip. Growing old, being in your 90s, is the hardest part of life, I think. You want to walk and run and do things, but every day you see yourself grow a little slower. You do less. Your friends die. Sometimes you wish you could just get on with it, too.

But then you have children, and they still need you. I worry about mine every day. My daughter is a lawyer in New York City and my son a doctor, who works on public policy issues in Washington, D.C.

And there are grandchildren as well. I want my grandchildren to know me and to have an idea of what life was like when I was young. Things have changed so much in my lifespan. Maybe it will be the same in theirs–maybe even more so.

I listen to the TV and radio, and they all seem to indicate that this could be a terrible time. But if I close my eyes and remember back, when I open them and see what we have today, I think, "This is heaven."

As a youngster in Kansas, I felt we had almost god-like powers when I first heard a voice speak out of a little box, or when we traveled in our Model T across a few miles of the Kansas prairie. Events and situations that boggled my mind in those days seem amusingly quaint today. It gives you some perspective on things.

One event I lived through still seems like a looming shadow un-paralleled in its darkness—the Depression. My grandchildren need to know about this, too, especially if we are going into tough times. These are times they have not seen, but I have. And my grandparents and great-grandparents lived through equally hard times. The kids need to know this, so they will not despair, should life turn harsh. Someday I may have great-grandchildren, too. I am writing this memoir for them as well. They can read it and know what my life was like back then.

I will be alive for them, but so will all the others. I want to bring all the others to life. Who are the others? Mother and Dad, of course. And my brother, Jim, and dear sister, Elsie Rene. My grandparents and, most of all, Great-Aunt Adaline; the quiet pioneer who helped me escape from an unhappy home. I want to bring them all to life.

August 2007

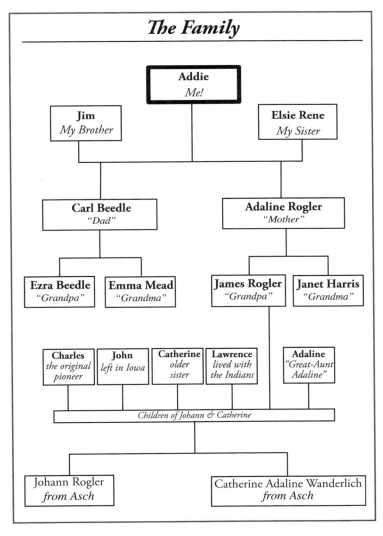

Addie age 3

Part I
My Childhood 1915-1924

1
August 8, 1915

They say times are going to be tough. Well, I was born in 1915 and, in the past 93 years, I have seen tough times. I've heard about even tougher–from my grandparents, who were early pioneers settling the Flint Hills of Kansas.

I had hoped my grandchildren, and their children, would never have to face serious adversities, but if they are called to do so I want them to know about their forebearers. Despite hardships we can barely imagine today, they built something. One, my loving and strong Great-Aunt Adaline, in her own quiet way, especially helped me.

Guess being in my 90s has set me to thinking how different things influenced my life. I really hadn't bothered to think this through before. Doubt there is any lesson I can utilize at my age, but my grandchildren and great-grandchildren might read my story and say, "Oh, that's happened to me!" Then, they might think differently about something.

This account of my journey is for them.

I was born on a farm in the Flint Hills of Kansas, in the midst of a severe drought. My Dad, a thin, sinewy man, loved to tell me about the day I was born. He did this many times when I was growing up; usually as we went around the house doing something casual together, like cooking breakfast. This is the story he told.

"Peaches," he would say, "You were born on August 8, 1915, on Great-Aunt Adaline's farm. I woke up early that day and as usual went out to the barn to milk the cow."

Dad would go on to explain that as he sauntered to the barn, he looked across the Flint Hills–a vast prairie-land formed when the east-central part of Kansas was covered with shallow seas. The Flint Hills are one of the world's best grazing regions when conditions are right. But this day, though young, was still, hot and windless. Dad thought of all that prehistoric water as he contemplated his uncertain crop. His gaze drifted to the empty river paths carved on the shallow valley bottoms.

At his feet, the earth's crust was cracked and sun-burnt. The tangled weeds and grass were brown from the drought. His crops stood short and withered. Rolling above the planting fields, like gentle swelling waves, the dung-colored hills were dotted with limestone and flint.

Dad worried about how little he had to pasture the animals on.

"I wished for rain," he always added with emphasis.

And then, as always in Chase County, Kansas, Dad saw the sky. A person walking in the Kansas Flint Hills is really aware of the sky; just like a person in New York sees tall buildings. Chase County is "big sky" country; you see the sky–you see it most. And it is a shifting, changing thing, like the sea for a sailor. It fills the field of vision.

"But, on August 8, 1915," Dad would continue, "it was brilliant blue and cloudless."

When Dad finished milking he returned to the house. There he strained the warm milk through a cheesecloth and took a glass to my mother, who waited for him in bed. She was 30 and he was 33 years old. As he told the story I knew that for many years to come this morning glass of milk would be part of their daily routine.

Mother was as soft and round as he was tough and lean. Her hair was golden blonde and her eyes were blue. Unusual for her day, Mother was educated. She went to Kansas State Teachers College in Emporia and studied journalism and music. She did some graduate work at the University of Kansas in Lawrence; maybe she even got a master's degree. I am not sure. She had an offer to work for *The Saturday Evening Post* in Philadelphia. But by that time she had met Dad. She wanted nothing more in life than to return home and marry him. And, after a trip to New York where she purchased the fabric for her wedding gown, she did just that.

She always loved that warm milk. There must have been a sense of tenderness between them, of future and growth. Mother was pregnant, with me.

Mother

Again, as he did every morning, Dad cooked breakfast for Mother and their three-year-old son, Jim.

That afternoon her labor pains started. The doctor, who lived about 10 miles away, was called. Funny, as I think of it now, I don't know how they called him—I doubt we had a phone at that time. I assume he came by horse or buggy. When the folks told me this story, I never thought to ask such things. Life when I was young was pretty much as it always was, and always had been.

Life was unchanged.

I never wondered about what the future might bring.

A neighbor lady came to help Mother and the doctor. She bathed and dressed me and put me in a rough wooden baby cradle with rockers. A pillow was my mattress. And so I started life.

I arrived at 10:00 p.m., with the life-giving rain. Hard, pouring, pounding rain. It rained until the fields were saturated. It rained until the roads were not safe for passage. The doctor had to stay overnight.

Dad told me I gave my family their 1915 crop!

I've always been proud that I brought the rain with me when I was born. My parents' very survival depended on it.

Addie as a baby

Like my mother, I was named Adaline after my mother's aunt Adaline, who owned the farm where I was born. I have no memory of living on that particular farm. Mother told a funny story about the place, however. Jim, my brother, was slow to walk but could make great strides on his hands and feet. One day Mother could not find him. She searched in a panic. Finally she found him on a silo, a tall round metal structure used to store animal feed. Always petite and rounded, Mother couldn't reach him no matter how she tried. A hired hand eventually brought the baby down. Thereafter, Mother tied a red bandanna handkerchief on Jim's head so she could see him more readily. Otherwise he remained free to roam the farm—a little boy exploring the barns and fields of Great-Aunt Adaline's farm.

The name Adaline did not stick on me at first. My brother Jim peered into my cradle. My skin was pink and my short hair yellow. I looked like peaches to him.

"Peaches" was my name for the next six years.

Dear Mother and Dad, did you suspect this new baby had the soul of a rebel? Did you ever dream what my life would be like? Or what the world would become 90 years later!

Today Chase County is scarcely populated. But things were different back when I was born. Then, close to 7,000 people lived in Chase County's 776 square miles, and their future looked bright. The wheat and cattle businesses were thriving. Both my Dad's and my Mother's families were prosperous. My cousin Albert Rogler was soon to be elected mayor of Cottonwood Falls, the county seat; his brother Henry Rogler was an accomplished rancher and a rising political star; my great-aunt Adaline Rogler and her husband, Nichol Gosler, were planning to donate land for our local schools. My father's family, the Beedles, was prosperous. Better still, by 1916 oil and gas leases were being taken throughout Chase County. People expected to strike it rich.

Moreover, the country was on the verge of a great economic boom. One year before I was born, in August 1914, a great war had broken out in Europe. Americans were actively selling wheat to Europe. Wheat prices shot up. They reached $1.60 a bushel the year I was born. Throughout World War I, the U.S. government guaranteed farmers $2.00 a bushel as their lowest price. Farmers throughout the Midwest increased production.

Progress was everywhere.

And the railroads were connecting the towns.

Walking the tracks, early 1900s

My brother Jim

2
Early Days

When I was three, we moved to a simple frame house in the nearby village of Bazaar. My first memories are of that house, that village, and World War 1.

Throughout the first months of my life, the war threat escalated. Germany began to develop her new weapon, the submarine, and with it to threaten American shipping. On May 17, 1915, a German submarine sank the *Lusitania*, a British ocean liner, killing many of the Americans on board. On April 6, 1917, President Wilson signed a resolution declaring war on Germany.

So my first memories arise just as Wilson was dedicating the whole of our country's economy to the production of goods for the war. It was an amazing accomplishment. Railroads were nationalized; flour was rationed; wheat was planted for the war effort. Farmers increased production as the Turkish navy blocked the grain from Russia that used to feed much of Europe.

With all this effort, it is no wonder the adults talked a lot about the war. I did not fully understand the words; but I clearly picked up the emotion and fear. I was afraid of the deadly threat if the Germans came to Bazaar. I spent days thinking, "What should I do?"

If the Germans arrived at out doorsteps I decided I needed a good place to hide. In those days, there were lots of horse-drawn wagons on the streets of Bazaar. If used for hay, they had slotted open sides. But nice, closed, box wagons were used to transport grain. One of these wagons would be a good place to hide, I decided. I felt safer with this plan.

Wheat Wagons, 1913

Jim and Addie

18

I also saw and heard about soldiers returning from the war—especially their condition when they came home, all shot up and hurt. I overheard one story that stuck with me forever.

A young Bazaar man had been to the front. He was sent home by railroad in a basket: blind, armless, and legless. His father met him at the Bazaar train station, pulled a pistol out, and shot him.

Dead.

When I heard this, a cold chill ran down my spine. But it lasted only a brief moment—a hair longer than the telling of the story itself. Kansas at that time was not a place for flailing about suffering. Death was a daily part of our lives. Children died frequently, mostly in the summer, from diarrhea. This was life.

Although I don't remember it, on January 12, 1918, German aliens were required to register at the central post office as a precaution against domestic sedition. Mother's family, the Roglers, had its roots in Germany. Americans of English ancestry looked with suspicion on "Germans," even if they, like the Roglers, had settled on the plains fifty or sixty years earlier and proudly raised their children as Americans. Feeling this sense of unease, my Rogler grandparents purchased three or four $1,000 U.S. savings bonds and glued them to their living room wall. No one would doubt their loyalty to this land. The bonds remained glued to the wall until one day many years later when my mother moved to the house and carefully soaked them off.

I clearly remember Armistice Day, November 11, 1918—the end of the war. The people of Bazaar celebrated by burning the Kaiser Wilhelm II in effigy. I wasn't sure what a "Kaiser" was, but I knew this was an exceptional event. The adults stuffed gunnysacks to look like a man and hung "him" from a high pole. The men in the crowd set "him" on fire. The blaze flashed and crackled against the evening sky. I was a little worried . . . was it a real man or not? I was uncertain how to react; but all the hard-working, good folks around me were happy, so in the end I was not too upset.

Aside from that exciting night, life continued its normal routine. Most of my time was spent out of doors running wild with my brother, Jim.

No one supervised us or seemed much concerned about what we did. We had no toys. We copied the hard-working adults in our lives.

We always had two wood burning stoves in our house—one that we used all year long in the kitchen and a living room stove that was moved into storage during the summer months. Dad kept a supply of wood close to the house to chop and use as needed.

One spring day when I was three, Jim and I decided to play at chopping firewood for the house stove. We frequently watched our thin, sinewy Dad chop a notch in a log and then saw the piece off the log. So, I picked up a small saw, and Jim, who was by then about six years old, picked up a double-bladed axe. We found a log.

I was to saw and Jim was to chop.

Somehow Jim got ahead of me. He started to chop before I had my turn. I was upset; going out of turn was not our game! Holding my turf, I forcefully bent to saw as he pulled the ax from the log.

The axe cut me deep over my right eye. Blood pulsing, I ran screaming into the house. Mother looked at the wound, said she saw the bone, pulled the two edges together, put some adhesive tape over the edges and sent me back outside to play. I can raise my hand above my eye and feel the scar today.

Jim, Addie, and the Speer family, Virginia, Aunt Elsie, and Junior in her arms

Jim and I also played "drilling for oil." With alarming frequency, Dad left home to seek his fortune in the oil fields that were opening all over Kansas. This seemed to excite the adults quite a lot. Everyone wanted to own an oil well!

Jim wanted to make an oil rig by wiring together three long sticks. My job was to hold the sticks while he climbed to the top. And so I did, for a moment. My strength gave way. Jim fell and tore a fingernail. Now it was his turn to run screaming to the house.

Mother repeated her therapy.

I also had my first earache in the house at Bazaar. I had no words to explain this painful sensation. I thought about it: what could it be? I told Mother that I had bumped my ear on the door. As pus began to ooze from the ear, she took me to the doctor. He told her to hold my head on her knees with the draining ear downward. The body warmth would soothe my pain, and gravity would help the pus come out. There were no antibiotics then.

I had many earaches in the years to come. I lost much of my hearing.

Other significant events, social and political, occurred while we lived in that house. About this time efforts were underway to give women the vote and to prohibit the drinking of alcohol. The role of women was to change tremendously during my lifetime; when I was young, throughout most of the United States, women couldn't vote and a married woman couldn't work.

Kansas may have been somewhat more progressive. In 1861 the state constitution granted women the right to own property and to have equal custody of their children. By 1912, women could vote in Kansas.

In 1889 Chase County's Cottonwood Falls elected a woman-run government, although it was just a joke that got out of control. As the local paper reported,

"The city of Cottonwood Falls attracts national attention by electing women to all city offices. It was begun as good-natured fun at the expense of the 'women-folks' but by noon the movement took on earnestness and try as they might the practical jokers could not stop it."

That was the way women were where I grew up. These were hard working women. They could influence the men-folk and one another. While the men worked the farm and tended to the cattle, or went off to drill for oil, the woman's role was just as essential to the survival, and economic well being, of the family.

The women raised the children, tended the garden and the chickens, kept the house, baked the food and, when the men needed help, pitched right in. Although the roles differed, these were full partners and strong women. No "shopping mall" wives there! If anything, as I will explain later, my family was somewhat unusual. My Rogler grandparents, having only two daughters, raised them to be somewhat "educated"–both were college graduates. Neither my mother nor my Aunt Elsie would go on to become typical farm wives.

In short, women, their role and voting, was something I was vaguely aware of at most. I thought nothing of it. It just was.

As for Prohibition, somehow there was more talk about it, or at least talk that stuck a chord with me. My Grandma Rogler wore a little Women's Christian Temperance Union pin showing she supported Prohibition. Grandma Beedle, my father's mother, used to recite a little ditty to me, "Lips that taste wine shall never touch mine." Because of these silly little things, I knew that both of my grandmothers actively supported Prohibition. Kansas was already a dry state when the Eighteenth Amendment became effective on January 19, 1920. Again, I never thought about what it meant, or whether there was another way.

I was more concerned with my daily life.

Since Dad was away so much, the times he came home stand out in my memory. These usually involved holidays. One Thanksgiving, on his way home, Dad purchased a goose for dinner without telling us. He brought the goose home under his arm in a sack, with its head sticking out. Mother and I were in the kitchen. As he walked in, the goose made a "big noise." I ran screaming from the room. I had never heard or seen anything like it. The adults had a laugh on my account, while Dad calmed me down and got me to pet it.

The next day Dad killed the goose. Then he plucked its feathers for a lovely down pillow and got it ready to cook. Boy did I enjoy eating that goose later for Thanksgiving dinner!

I also remember Christmas Eve 1918. Again, Dad came home from the oil fields. This time he made us candy—my first taste of candy. It was fondant flavored with lemon. I think it was made with sugar, water, and cream of tartar to keep the syrup from crystallizing. I watched, not certain what to expect, as my stringy father bent over the boiling pot and stirred till the syrup cooled in the pan. Through a mysterious alchemy, the liquid hardened into something sweet and solid. I loved it!

When I was four we moved about a mile out of Bazaar to a house on the main road that connected Cottonwood Falls with Matfield Green, a small village where my mother's grandparents had settled in the 1860s. The move to Bazaar changed our house, but not Mother's parental skills. No matter how sick, we children were always sent outside to play. One winter day, Jim and I were coughing and vomiting. Mother made us spaghetti with tomato sauce for lunch, and then put us in our coats to play outside. I can still remember the red tomatoes and spaghetti we vomited on the snow as we threw snowballs at one another. We had the whooping cough.

The road between Cottonwood Falls and Matfield Green, two dusty ruts, ran by the front of our house. Deep drainage pipes ran underneath the grade of the road from time to time. These were designed to protect the road from our infrequent but heavy rains by carrying turbulent waters under the roadbeds and out into the fields (which frequently flooded in any event). Although I was young I intuitively understood that those pipes were dangerous when channeling the rapidly flowing runoff from a heavy rain.

Traffic was light in those days, and I mostly associate the road with Jim's daily walk of about a mile to school. Jim walked alone. But one spring day, when I was four, Mother and I walked along with Jim for the first time. I did not know why. Still, I was happy for the change.

When we arrived at the schoolhouse, Mother asked the teacher if I, a four-year old, could attend first grade. "Yes," was the answer. Now that I'm old, I love to learn. But back then I wasn't that interested in learning. In any event, I don't remember learning anything. Instead, I remember walking home in the uncertain weather, and one walk in particular.

The rain and wind were strong as we walked home that day. Hardy as we were, Jim and I got to a point where we could go no further. On the open prairie there was no place to seek shelter as the agitated winds whipped around us. Wet and cold, we climbed inside a drainage pipe to get warm. There we huddled together. And then came the pouring flood–of anger. Why didn't Mother leave the house to seek us out? I wished mightily that I had the kind of mother who would come to meet her children in a bad storm.

Sometimes I think now, "What a miracle that I survived." But we all did. Mother never lost a child.

Somewhere about this time, Dad bought a black Model T Ford to drive to Cottonwood Falls–no more buggy! I think it cost about $100.

It was quite a contraption of cranks and levers that had to be adjusted frequently and none of which responded all that quickly. I remember Dad cranking to start it up. It had pedals on the floor and a gas lever on the steering wheel. We never went near the car unless Dad was there–it was a very special thing. It could go up to 20 miles an hour, at a time when a good horse could hit 4-5 miles per hour.

Just outside Cottonwood Falls there was a steep hill. When the car came to the hill, all the passengers except Dad got out. Then Dad turned the car around and backed it up the hill. Dad said the car didn't have enough power to climb the hill in forward gear.

Walking up the hill didn't matter to me; as far as I was concerned, we enjoyed unimaginable, and almost god-like, power. Looking back now, it all seems slightly quaint.

Cottonwood Falls was also a treat and a place of great sophistication in my young mind. It was a town of about 1,000 people! If you needed to buy something, you pretty much went to Cottonwood Falls to buy it. It was the county seat. And as a result, Chase County built a fancy courthouse there, modeled on French designs. It was the finest building I could imagine. Also in Cottonwood Falls, there were a doctor, judges, and lawyers, and stores with fancy clothes. There were barbershops and cattlemen congregated around the railroad station just outside town. The prosperous times continued to roll. In the summer of 1919, wheat was bringing over $2.06 per bushel.

We also used the Model T when we drove to visit relatives, mostly on holidays.

During Christmas 1919, Dad drove us to visit Mother's mother and father, the Roglers, in Matfield Green in their little house with the U.S. savings bonds pasted on the living room wall.

That Christmas, Grandma Rogler made candleholders out of Irish potatoes, carving a hole in the center to hold the candle and carving a design on the outside. She placed these on the dining table. In the evening she lit the candles and their light cast a festive glow. I was so proud of how clever my grandma was. This pride was reinforced with the knowledge that she was a college graduate, and education always mattered in the Rogler family.

Grandma and Grandpa Rogler, their children and grandchildren (Addie in top row, held by Mother)

A few months later we drove to the Rogler farm again. This time a baseball game was underway. These were played on the community pasture, a short distance from the Rogler homestead, where people could keep their cattle for $5 a season. When the games were played, the cattle just gravitated to the far end of the pasture.

At that time, and for years after, the men from nearby villages frequently played against one another and the games were a great source of entertainment to the whole community. The Matfield Green team was spearheaded by a former minor league player, who at the time also worked as the janitor for the local school. The games were always heavily attended by the local communities–with "crowds" of 20 or 30 people watching.

On this particular day there was extra excitement. An airplane pilot, seeing the crowd, landed on the pasture. The pilot jumped out of his two-seater and offered to take people on a flight. Each flight cost five dollars.

Grandma Rogler was thrilled. She announced that she would take a flight as soon as she had saved the money to do so. She was the only adult who wanted to fly. And she eagerly awaited the arrival of the plane on its subsequent visit. She never took that flight.

I have these memories of Grandma Rogler, and one more.

In June 1920, we drove once again to visit Mother's parents in Matfield Green.

On June 6, the morning after we arrived, Grandma Rogler went to her garden to pick peas for dinner. She sat shelling peas in the kitchen and talking to Mother, who was washing the breakfast dishes. I, as usual, goofed around outside playing. I was enjoying looking at the flowers and trees around the house, and listening to the birds sing.

In the midst of this uneventful morning scene, Grandma paused in her shelling.

She calmly said, "I feel rather queer. I believe I–"

She fell to the floor.

When I came inside, Grandma was on the kitchen floor with a pillow under her head.

I was confused. This was an unusual sight.

In the next second, I realized Mother was on the phone. I can still see that phone. It hung on the living room wall and had a crank.

Mother was frantically talking to someone—it was a doctor. I started crying. Dad came in, gathered me up, took me outdoors, and placed me on a swing. I fell out, skinning my knees.

There was a lot of commotion, and my role was simply to stand by and watch, it seemed.

At this time people were buried from their homes. Grandma Rogler, as was customary, had a three-day wake, with family and friends sitting with her body day and night. Her two daughters, Mother and Aunt Elsie, three years younger, took turns sitting by her side. The coffin was open. Usually during the night a couple of people would sit together and quietly chat the time away.

"Mother," I asked, "do we sit up to show our respect?"

"Yes," she told me, and also to make sure that rats and mice did not come out to gnaw the body. We lived in simply constructed wood frame homes, and I often saw the little black pellets of mice droppings and the occasional poor mouse, flattened in our spring traps. Rats clearly frequented the barn, where we kept our grain.

"I guess making sure that nothing bothers her is a sign of respect," Mother concluded.

On the third day a preacher came to the home and gave a sermon.

We were not a particularly religious family, and the area was not affluent enough to attract an abundance of preachers, so our religion was as simple and spare as our wood frame homes. We were "Christian," whatever distinctions beyond this existed, and that was that. On Sundays one of the townsfolk conducted the services, with a traveling preacher coming on occasion.

Somehow a "real" preacher was obtained for Grandma Rogler's funeral. Since the preacher probably didn't know her, his sermon was about "the departed." I was so stuck by this name for my grandmother—the departed—that I don't recall anything else he said.

She was placed in the lime-laden earth of the Matfield Green cemetery.

I try to think about what I knew of Grandma Rogler. Mostly, she has faded from my memory.

Thinking back about her now with the perspective that age brings, I know another thing. Grandma Rogler did not raise a typical farm family for her day. Most families were large, 10 to 12 children being common, with sons to help on the farm. Grandma Rogler had only two children—both girls. Her first, my mother, was born when she was 26 years old. This was an old age in those days, when girls mostly were married in their teens. Did she use some form of birth control? I will never know, we almost never spoke of such things when I was young.

Also, the education of her girls mattered to Grandma Rogler. The emphasis on education, especially for the daughters, was very unusual during that day and age. However, in her case this was not a surprise. Grandma graduated from Cincinnati's Farmer's College and taught school in various locations before landing in Chase County. There, while teaching at the Brandley school, she met Grandpa.

When Grandma's eldest daughter, my Mother, finished grade school, the family moved to Cottonwood Falls so that the girls could attend high school. Throughout the family's stay in Cottonwood Falls Grandpa worked in a stone quarry that supplied blocks for houses. The girls continued their education, both going on to college. After both their girls finished college, my grandparents moved back to live on their farm. The education of their girls was all-important to them.

Aside from these snippets, I suspect that the little else I remember about Grandma Rogler comes mostly from family pictures. These show her dark brown hair parted neatly down the middle and framing her broad calm face. When I think of her, the words "pleasant" and "caring" come to mind, and "attractively rounded." Not much more.

Grandma Rogler with grandchildren

My Grandmother's Mother, Deborah Harris

Here is a little bit more about Grandma Rogler's family that I have heard from various sources over the years. Grandma Rogler was the daughter of Leonard B. and Deborah (Jennings) Harris, of Cincinnati, Ohio. Her parents were married on April 14, 1844, and may have been second cousins. Janet was raised by one of her mother's sisters in Kansas because her mother died of childbed fever when she was born. Leonard Harris married again; his second wife and their ten children all died of tuberculosis.

Family tradition has it that Leonard's Harris ancesters came from England to Richmond, Virginia, in the 1600s, where they were merchants. During the Revolution they were Tories; when the war ended they fled to Cincinnati.

Adaline and Elsie

Adaline and Elsie reading

Adaline, my Mother, at school (second from right in front row)

Matfield Green stockyards

3
Matfield Green

After Grandma Rogler died, Grandpa Rogler was left alone. Somehow the adults decided that our family should take care of him. By September of 1920 the farm economy was beginning to slump. Maybe this influenced the grownups' discussions. In any event in 1920, we moved to Grandpa Rogler's farm and lived in the wooden house with the savings bonds pasted on the wall. Grandpa had built this house for Grandma Rogler just before they were married.

It had five rooms.

The front door opened right into the living room. That door was never used. Everyone used the door off the screened-in back porch, always. Even for Grandma's funeral. We were that kind of casual people.

The simply furnished living room was full of books and magazines. We always had the Sears catalogue and a daily newspaper published in Topeka, which the family avidly read. Besides a couch and chairs, the living room had a linoleum floor that was damp mopped every morning to take off the gritty dust. There was a potbellied stove in the living room during the cold months. It was stored in the root cellar when the weather turned warm. Just before our family moved in, a single bed was set up in a corner of the living room. This would be Grandpa's bed from then on. On one wall of the living room, the U.S. government bonds my grandparents had purchased during World War I were still prominently displayed. After we moved in Mother soaked the U.S. savings bonds off the wall. I guess she wanted some other decoration up there. Or maybe the family was not doing so well and she needed to find a way to redeem them. I am not sure.

The telephone was on the wall by the living room, the one I remembered Mother using to call the doctor when Grandma died. All calls were made through party lines. To call someone on your line you turned a crank on the side of the phone. This caused all the phones on the line to ring. People could tell whether the call was for them or not by the sound of the ring. Our ring was 5 short rings–about two cranks for each ring. A long ring was double the cranks of a short ring. Each house on the party line had a unique short, long combination for its ring. To reach anyone not on the party line, you called the central station in Matfield; there, the local operator connected you to the desired person's home phone.

Behind the living room was a kitchen and dining area with a round table, and the entrance to the screened porch, where we entered and left the house. Three bedrooms were off the dining area. Years later, in the 1940s or 50s, a pantry off the kitchen became the indoor bathroom.

Off the screened porch we had a wonderful honeysuckle bush and, a few steps beyond, a little wooden outhouse. We kept this stocked with Montgomery Ward and Sears Roebuck catalogues to use as toilet paper. At night inside we also had pots for an emergency. But no one wanted to use them, or to be the one to empty and clean them in the morning. I have to say this nasty task fell to Mother.

There was no electricity. We read by the light of gasoline lamps if Dad was home. Dad would burn the ash wicks to just the right point so that they would glow. He also knew how to mix the gasoline with air. Mother was afraid of the gasoline lamps, which had to be carefully maintained. When Dad was away, Mother used kerosene lamps, even though their chimneys had to be washed every morning to get the soot off. She kept three or four around the living room, one on a wall and the rest on the tables. We went to bed in the dark, or used a flashlight. Electricity did not arrive in our house until the 1940s.

On the same side of the house as the honeysuckle bush, wooden doors led to the cellar. When he built the wooden frame, Grandpa Rogler dug out the cellar under the house and lined it with an arched stone roof to protect his family in case the house above blew away. Every house in Kansas has a cellar like this, because Kansas is in the middle of "cyclone alley." Our cool cellar walls were lined with jars of canned goods, and it was used for other kinds of storage as well, such as potatoes and turnips in the winter.

This is the house to which Grandma Rogler came as a young bride. This is the house where she gave birth to her daughters—Mother and Aunt Elsie. This is the house where she died and where my sister was born.

Mother loved this house and the views of the sky, fields and gardens from its windows. An avid reader as a young girl, she named the farm "Tanglewood" after reading *Tanglewood Tales for Boys and Girls* (1853) written by Nathaniel Hawthorne. In the introduction, Hawthorne describes his love for a "humble" roof that "I could really call my own" with views that others might find "tame"; but which worked their "quiet charm" in "broad meadows and gentle eminences." He wished for a lifetime of discovery "among green meadows and placid slopes, with outlines forever new."

Mother knew an apt description of her home, hills and meadows when she saw it. She closed the book and told her father that the family homestead should be called "Tanglewood." He went along with it. To others in our little village it was "the Rogler homestead," or in later years, "the Beedle farm." To Mother it was "Tanglewood." Growing up, I knew of the name and that the source had been a book. I thought maybe Shakespeare, but no one read *Tanglewood Tales* to me or thought to give me a copy to read myself.

The living room windows of our Tanglewood overlooked a garden, and then wide, gentle rolling fields of waving grain. You could see for miles. Off the porch there was another lower field, often planted in corn, and then acres of orchard planted with fruit trees—apples, peaches, cherries, and apricots that looked especially beautiful when blooming in the spring. The bedroom windows opened onto flowering bushes, the back field and our clothesline. And, of course, as I mentioned earlier, everyplace you saw the sky; whatever its color, whatever the clouds. Mother had a cousin, Emily, also a schoolteacher, who lived nearby. In the early summer evenings we would hear the five short rings on our phone and know it was Emily calling Mother to say, "Look out your west window at that beautiful sunset." Then they chatted about family and politics.

"I was born here and I will die here," Mother always said. In 1971, so many years later, she did. It was a very special place to her.

As we were growing up, Mother repeatedly told us a story to underscore why our house in Matfield Green was so very special.

Here it is.

As I mentioned earlier, Grandma Rogler had two children, Mother and Elsie, who was three years younger. Never were two sisters less alike than these two. Mother had blue eyes and straight golden-blonde hair. Aunt Elsie had brown eyes and curly dark-brown hair. Grandma Rogler was dark like Aunt Elsie. Mother liked to sit and read and think. She liked to be waited on. Aunt Elsie liked to be active and care for other people. Mother loved the world of ideas. Aunt Elsie, equally educated but somehow more sophisticated, liked the world of fashion.

One day, when her daughters were young, Grandma Rogler took Aunt Elsie and Mother by train to Cincinnati to see their grandfather Leonard Harris. Mother always started the story by reminding us of how different she looked from her dark-haired mother and sister.

On the train ride to Ohio, Grandma Rogler corrected Mother for something she did. Mother heard a near-by passenger say, "She must be a stepchild."

Mother always told us about the stepchild comment. It must have struck a deep chord in her heart that underscored her difference from her mother and her sister. However, that was not the real point of the story, or at least not the only one.

The real point was that Mother didn't like Leonard's house in Ohio. She said it had rugs and heavy drapes that made the house dark. I suspect it was a fashionable house; something my mother would have been deeply uncomfortable with. Throughout the brief visit, Mother wanted to go back home to Matfield Green, with its simple ways and light-filled horizons.

Mother repeated this story to us children frequently as we grew up, always emphasizing the unhappiness of leaving Matfield Green; only recently I realized she never told us what her grandfather was like—not even his name! As an adult I have wondered about him and found out a bit about his life. The purpose of the story in Mother's mind was as a vehicle to instruct her children frequently and in detail about the contrast between our house and the dark houses of Cincinnati: Mother always kept the sun shining through the windows in our house, using blinds and light curtains. She loved to see the endless views of the Flint Hills and the sky, her garden and the iridescent hummingbirds darting in her hollyhocks, and so forth. Fate would draw us away from Matfield in the years to come, and each time Mother was heart-breakingly homesick. After hearing this story maybe a thousand times, only a curious child, like me, dared to think of leaving our flinty hills for an uncertain, but different, life amid the "gloom" of the outside world.

So, now, with Grandma's untimely death, the family moved to Mother's childhood home in Matfield Green. Mother was thrilled.

Great-Aunt Adaline feeding chickens; Mother has captioned the photo "Tanglewood"

That first summer, Grandpa planted sweet corn down in the field closest to the house–the one between the house and the orchard. I watched as he prepared a special area with his horse and plow. Then, his fine-boned frame bent over a wooden corn planter and his bushy eyebrows squinted to block out the sun as he dropped a few grains at a time into the furrows. Every two weeks he planted another furrow or two, so that the sweet corn would ripen throughout the summer. One day, thumping the porch door shut as he walked inside, he took off his floppy and sweat-stained hat, wiped his brow and made an offer to Jim and me. If over the summer we picked and delivered the corn about a half a mile walk to the village, we could keep the money. We squealed with delight at the thought of that money.

When the corn was ready to eat, Jim and I knocked on doors in the village–a light sprinkling of clapboard houses around the main crossroad. Three hundred people lived there. At each door we took orders for delivery the next day. We sold the corn for 10 cents a dozen, delivered. Every morning, we went to the patch, picked the sweet corn, put it in our little red wagon, and delivered it. This lasted until we both started back in school in September.

As Grandpa promised, we were allowed to keep the money we made. We collected over $10 that summer. I never thought of spending a cent. I thought only about saving the money, which I did in a cigar box. I hid the box in the large closet in my parents' room. The closet had several shelves and a row of wooden hooks on which the clothes were hung. A few wire hangers also hung off the hooks, with some of the better clothes on them. One particular shelf was used to store quilts, comforters, and other bedding. They nicely covered the cigar box and hid it from view. I checked our money every week and sometimes more frequently. It made me feel secure to see all that cash!

That first summer, and every summer thereafter on the Rogler homestead, we slept on folding cots under a stand of cedar trees. The house was located on a cliff, overlooking the cornfield and these trees stood just in front of the cliff. They smelled beautiful, and their shade was so welcome on a hot sunny day. Dad usually set the cots up, with a pillow and a sheet to pull over us. We left everything set up outside all summer long–unless rain was coming. Then we had to dash around to bring the cots and bed stuff in. This added a fine element of excitement

Elsie and Adaline out for a drive

to the day, and after the rain you could always enjoy the steel smell of ozone in the air.

While the summer rains fell, Jim and I danced and played outside, relishing the cool heavy feeling of clothes plastered against our thin bodies. After the rain stopped, we kept the wet clothes on. As they dried, they cooled us during the heat of the summer day.

My children sometimes ask if I was afraid to sleep outdoors. The answer is no, we were outdoors children. I don't remember any harm coming to us, in any event. Sometimes Dad sprayed the area for mosquitoes. But he never did anything to protect us from animals. Beaver were there. They never left the water stream. The raccoons and skunks stayed in the timber areas. Buffalo, deer, and antelope once were plentiful on our land. They had been killed off by the time we moved to the homestead.

We had a black dog, Jeff, whom we dearly loved. He pulled our little red wagon and spent lots of time barking if a Model T car drove past. He also slept outside with us. (Dogs were never allowed into the house.) So maybe he helped keep the animals at bay.

There were lots of different trees on our place—oak, sycamore, cottonwood, walnut, elm, cedar and maple. We constantly fought to keep the timberland in check. The black walnut trees were among my favorites. Jim and I gathered the nuts in the fall after the frost, when both leaves and nuts lay scattered on the ground.

Cracking the shells, which we did with a hammer, was hard work, but the taste of the black walnuts contained a wonderful hint of the candy and cakes Mother would later make with those nuts. The best trees on the place, however, were on the five south acres.

Mother planted fruit trees there; the apples, peaches, cherries and apricots I mentioned. In the spring we could see acre upon acre of blossoms. Later in the season, people came from all over to pick their own fruit, and my parents became well known for this.

Nestled in my outdoor cot, under the trees, I would look at the golden light in the Flint Hills–like a pail of pure radiance poured from heaven. I loved the sunsets and sunrises and the full moons. At night I could look across to see our corn in the lower field tipped with silver light.

When we slept outside, a dense canopy of stars set the sky aglow. As moonlight washed across the sky, I looked up from my cot and thought, with a fine feeling of well being, how beautiful my world was. I was a small, trusting speck and filled with the wonder of the night. I never thought beyond my world or of places far away. Later in the evening, I loved to look at the Big Dipper and the shining moon. I made many a "wish upon a star."

Star light, star bright.
First star I see tonight.
Wish I may, wish I might
Have the wish I wish tonight.

I recall saying that little ditty frequently, but I don't remember a single wish I made as a child.

Now, if I were to make a wish, it would be to win the New York State mega-million lottery. Never heard of this as a child; it didn't even exist then.

How things have changed!

Jim and our wagon

After we moved up with Grandpa, women started to wear their hair short. Mother's hair was long, very thick, and a beautiful golden-blonde color. She decided to wear it short. One Saturday evening she asked Dad to walk with her to the barbershop in Matfield Green. She was going to cut her hair. When they returned they were laughing and holding hands. Mother's hair was now ear-length.

The folks giggled about how the barber hadn't wanted to cut it; he thought her hair was so beautiful. Mother insisted. The barber did as he was told, but bawled the whole time. When he was done he carefully wrapped up her beautiful braid of hair and gave it to her in case she regretted cutting it. I don't think she did. Mother wore the exact same ear-length hairstyle for the rest of her life. I think she just found it easier to care for it short; and she always cared more about matters of the mind than her appearance.

During this period, the farm economy continued to weaken. Warren G. Harding was elected president. His campaign slogan was "Less government in business, and more business in government." He embarked on a series of initiatives to return the country to "normal" times, primarily by encouraging unfettered business activities. So while the farm economy weakened, the railroads and mines flourished. Dad spent less time farming and more time away from home in the oil fields and mines of the American west.

On January 28, 1921, I woke up to find I had a new sister, Elsie Rene. She was the most beautiful baby sleeping in my old cradle. I was delighted! Her arrival was a complete surprise to me. Mother, who did not care one whit about style, always wore shapeless dresses with a sugar sack tied as an apron. The sack was held above her breasts with strings and tied at the back. She tended to be heavy. I never realized Mother was pregnant, or knew what that might mean.

I assumed the doctor brought us this lovely baby. This belief was confirmed by a subsequent discovery.

Shortly after Elsie Rene's arrival, I went to check on Jim and my corn money. It was missing. I ran to tell Mother. She was unperturbed.

"Oh, we needed the money to pay the doctor for Elsie Rene," she casually said.

Now my suspicions were confirmed: Mother and Dad bought Elsie Rene from the doctor. I was delighted with Elsie Rene and, as far as I can recall, I was no longer upset about the money. From the moment she left the cradle, Elsie Rene and I slept together in a double bed. She was my great friend till the day she died seventy-two years later.

In the early days, however, Elsie Rene developed colic and cried long hours every evening. We rocked her in the cradle. Grandpa Rogler rocked her the hardest and the best. Then he sang to her.

Sleep baby, sleep.
Thy father is watching the sheep.
Thy mother is shaking the dreamland trees.
Down falls a little dream on thee.
Sleep baby, sleep.

Elsie Rene was quiet when Grandpa Rogler rocked her.

At first they used to bathe her in a basin on the kitchen table. Later, when she was two or three years old, she was bathed in a round metal clothes tub, same as Jim and me. Mother used rainwater to wash

Elsie Rene's hair. I still remember how soft and sweet and pink she was to look at. Mother breast-fed her for a year, as she did with Jim and me.

When Elsie Rene started to talk, she called me "Ping." Thus ended "Peaches." Ping was my name at home for years until I protested and insisted on being "Adaline." I don't know why, but I was the only one of the three children that had a nickname.

During this time at the Rogler homestead, Jim and I learned

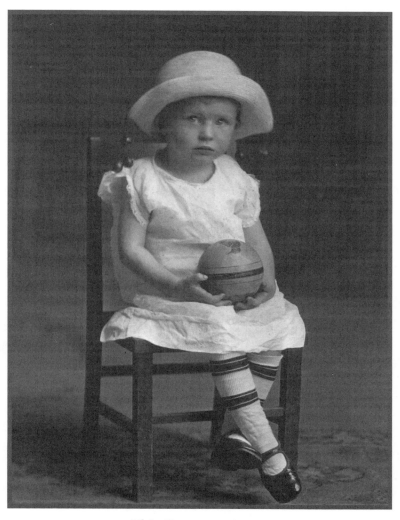

Elsie Rene, my sister

about chores. Jim, long-limbed and strong as a colt, worked right along with the men. With a weathered cowboy hat sheltering his sunburnt head, he fed the pigs, helped with the cattle, and was always busy farming. This was what boys did; they quickly grew into men's work.

Elsie Rene, unlike other farm girls, never had a chore to do. Only rarely did she even help dry the dishes. Even when she was older she simply stayed in the house and read along with Mother. Maybe Mother told her about *Tanglewood Tales* during one of those sessions? I will never know.

I never resented Elsie Rene, though–she was always just special. Now I recognize that the way Mother raised her had repercussions when she grew up. She married a farm boy, Melvin. He expected his wife to take care of the chickens, garden, and bake bread like every other farm wife. The first year of their marriage they lived on a ranch and Elsie Rene taught but did not do any farm work. It must have been a stormy period. Recognizing that his wife was not going to take on a typical woman's role, Melvin moved the family to town.

"It's lucky that I loved her so much," he once told me. In town Elsie Rene was an excellent housewife, but with no chickens or garden. Like Mother, she was not raised to be your usual farm wife.

Maybe I was. But it was not going to stick.

My first chores were to feed the chickens, gather the eggs,

Jim, Dad holding Elsie Rene and Addie

44

and clean the hen house. The hen house had poles where the chickens roosted. Underneath these were "dropping boards." Periodically the boards needed to be cleaned. The droppings were put on the garden as fertilizer. I did this.

I also had to clean the chickens' water containers and fill them morning and evening, then shell a large metal bucket of corn in the barn and carry it to the chicken areas, morning and evening. We had a metal contraption to help shell the corn. You put an ear of corn into a slot and turned a wheel–corn kernels fell into the bucket and the cob came out the other side.

I also made sure there was oyster shell in the dispenser so that the hens would lay eggs with hard shells. Dad bought this at a store in Cottonwood Falls.

Every evening I gathered eggs from the nests in the hen house. The eggs were shipped in cases to wholesalers in Kansas City or taken to the village and sold to the local store. My job was important. The eggs usually paid for our groceries–things like coffee, sugar, and flour.

We raised most of our other foods–all the vegetables, meat, and fruit. Usually we ate just what was in season, except during the winter. Then, we ate whatever fruits and vegetables Mother had canned earlier that year.

I used to watch her can. The method depended on what was being canned. Tomatoes, and some fruits that were acidic, would be washed, quartered, and cooked. The "cans"–glass jars really–were sterilized in a pot of boiling water. When the jars were steaming hot, she pulled them out with tongs and put them on a pie tin with a towel on it. Using a sterilized ladle she scooped the tomatoes in, placed a rubber circle around the rim and screwed on a metal ring to hold in place a flat metal lid. The she turned the jar upside down to make sure that nothing came out around the lid–if this happened she would tighten the ring further.

Mother would make as many cans as she had food on hand. Sometimes she had as many as 13-14 quarts a day to put up. Dad loved her tomato preserves, peeled and chopped tomatoes with lots of sugar, cloves and lemon slices. This was boiled till it was real thick. Dad used it on toast, and sometimes on the meat he was eating.

Addie with her 4H project

Jim with his 4H project

There was another way of canning, which we used when the food to be canned had no acid–things like vegetables and meat. This was more work. For these she filled the cans first. With meat, she would cut it up, sometimes brown it a bit and put in a little water. Then the jars were cooked in the water pressure cooker. Maybe they cooked a half hour or so. When the time was up, she would let the pressure go down, tighten the lids down and check for leaks. Then they were done.

When these jars were cool, we kids carried them to the storm cellar where there would be row upon row lining the shelves. It amounted to hundreds of cans–this was our winter food. Anything we grew, Mother canned.

Let me tell you, if you wanted to eat fruits and vegetables in the winter, you canned during the summer. I liked the canned fruits better than the canned vegetables.

In the springtime, every now and then, a hen would be sitting on its nest. When I approached, these hens clucked and pecked at me. Mother called these "setting hens" because they wanted to stay on the eggs in their nest to hatch their chicks. Mother took them off the nests and confined them to a small area. Eventually they stopped clucking and returned to "normal" activity.

Mother placed some of these fertilized eggs in incubators that we kept in our cellar. The incubators were simply boxes placed above a kerosene lamp that gave off warmth as it burned. Mother put an X on one side of each fertilized egg. Each day she turned the eggs so that the baby chicks developed properly. She carefully tended to the wick, keeping the eggs at a uniformly warm temperature. After about three weeks, the baby chicks pecked through their shells.

I did not view the baby chicks as cute or fun. I viewed them as food and life and money for survival. I knew that it would take the soft yellow balls about two months to turn into chickens that we could eat. And that is what amazed me.

Mother would kill the chickens and prepare them for cooking. Most women did that by holding the chicken by its legs and wings and chopping its head off with an axe. Mother, however, was afraid that she would hurt herself with the axe; so instead she put the chicken's head on the ground, firmly planted her foot on the head, and pulled. The head would just come off.

Next she scalded the chicken in hot water, picked off its feathers, and saved the soft feathers from its breast to make down pillows. To get off any remaining pinfeathers, she took the bird outside, matched a cone of newspaper and "singed" the skin, burning the thin feathers off.

Then, she would flour and season the pieces and fry them in a deep pan. It filled the house with the most delicious smell. We would have hot chicken for the noon meal and cold for the evening. Without refrigeration, the chickens were our main source of fresh meat during the summer. I always enjoyed those meals.

The process of producing food was such a daily imperative; I readily understood the role that the eggs, the chicks and the chickens played in our survival.

After the chicks hatched, we moved them to the brooder house, a small 10 × 10 foot building located in the northwestern corner of our yard. In the middle of the brooder house was a stove with a metal umbrella over it to reflect heat and keep the baby chicks warm. When the chicks had feathers and could keep themselves warm, they left the brooder house to run and flutter in a little pen attached to it.

At this stage my role in the family food chain began in earnest. The pen was near a row of cottonwood trees where blue jays nested. When the baby chicks were turned out into the open pen, the blue jays swooped down onto the chicks' backs. Then the jays used their strong bills to pick out the little chicks' brains. The jays were rapid in the dive and only took a second to pick that brain out, leaving a little clean opening and an empty skull. It was my job to shoo the jays off. Their dives were so fast, no matter how hard I tried, they always got at least one chick before I could get there. Its soft, yellow downy covering would be pierced and there would be a hole cleaned out. The brain would be gone.

In the morning after tending to the eggs and chicks, I walked into town to shop and picked up the mail for my family and Great-Aunt Adaline. At this time, she lived close to us in the town of Matfield Green, where she and her husband also owned several other houses that they rented out. They also were involved in our little local bank, where her husband was the cashier. I would carry a pail with ten dozen or so eggs in it as I walked the dirt road to town. I was going to exchange the eggs for flour, sugar and coffee. These were usually the only store-bought groceries the family needed, everything else we provided for ourselves.

The Snedegar family owned a store in Matfield and it served as both the local grocery and post office. When you walked in there was a long thick wooden counter on the right-hand side. The first thing I always noticed was the candy–a great case with trays of candy bars, candy corn and peppermints. Mother let me have 5 cents a week and I frequently used this to buy a chocolate bar. Mr. Snedegar, or Mrs. Snedegar, if she was minding the store, would put my pail of eggs on the counter, count them out and place them in an open wire basket for the other customers to buy them. This wire basket was kept on the far end of the counter. Above and behind the counter there were shelves of groceries, including some canned goods. Of course, the store had no electricity and no refrigeration. There was no way to buy meat or butter. Milk, however, could be purchased in cans.

The Snedegars kept an open account of the price they paid for the eggs and what the folks owed them for the groceries. Every once in a while they would settle with my parents.

Having concluded my business, I would ask for the mail. Mr. Snedegar always manned the post office, which was in the back of the building. Also in the back there was a pot-bellied stove and some arm chairs arround a spittoon. Here the village men spent their free time in neighborly conversation during the winter months.

Matfield Green, 1900s

On Saturday nights Snedegar's and the other little local grocery and dry goods store, Largent's, stayed open late–9 o'clock as I recall. Then the village people and those on the surrounding farms came to town, all neat and clean (but still in work clothes), to shop and visit. The local farmers often used this as the time to buy a week's supply of provisions. In the summer the shoppers would sit on the benches outside the stores, and in the winter they would sit by the stoves; they would stand and chat and wait for orders to be filled. It was a low-key but important social occasion.

Looking back it was amazing how self-sufficient our little village was. We did not rely on the outside for food, nor for entertainment. Like most of the rural villages around us, we were mostly self-contained. We never dreamed of what our country might become, or of receiving foodstuff from across the ocean.

As I dropped off Great-Aunt Adaline's mail, I would chat with her for a few minutes. She was my Grandfather's youngest sister, and one of the original pioneers–coming to Chase County as a young girl in a covered wagon. I loved to talk with her. Sometimes she told me stories about the past when there were bands of Indians wandering the land and how she was hidden from them in a rotten tree stump. Other times she told me how her family came to Kansas from Germany, in the end driving a covered wagon over dried up riverbeds as they proceeded into the heart of a searing drought. These were short, simple conversations, imparting just a bit of the family's history each time.

Having taken a break through my conversation with Great-Aunt Adaline, I proceeded home to my afternoon chores. Back at home I would hoe and weed the garden. The water supply came from a spring located northeast of the house. I could walk and carry a pail. I could help get the water.

I can never remember saying to Mother, "I have nothing to do."

Even our "recreational" activities were utilitarian. Jim and I both belonged to the 4H Club. The four H's stood for head, heart, hands, and health. The club taught us useful practical skills. Jim raised pigs, and I raised chickens; just like every other boy and girl in the county, with possibly the only exception being my sister Elsie Rene.

Sometime during this period we were to go to Cottonwood Falls for Grandpa Beedle's birthday party. I decided that Elsie Rene and

I needed haircuts for the occasion. Dad usually cut my hair by sitting me on a chair and giving me his "standard" haircut–straight all around my head. Sometimes the kids at school teased me about it. They said it looked like a bowl had been put on top of my head and the hair cut all around. I looked at the other girls, with their hair cut in bangs and shoulder length, and it just got me irritated. We couldn't afford a barber, so this was how my hair looked. And Dad never used a bowl, just his eye. Anyhow, in preparation for the big party I decided to do the cutting myself.

I put a pillow on a chair and lifted Elsie Rene up on it. She sat still while I cut her hair. Then I combed my hair and, watching in a hand mirror, cut my bangs. A big triangle wedge fell to the floor. I realized that this was not what I had intended and stopped.

Mother was horrified. They had been planning to take a family picture, she said shaking her head, and I had ruined it. Dad cut my bangs short so that the wedge was not so deep. But it was still noticeable.

Well, we dressed and went to the party. When everyone saw my haircut they decided not to take a family picture. Still, I was happy. At least no one had yelled at me.

That first September in Matfield Green, I started attending the local village schoolhouse built on the land donated by Great-Aunt Adaline and her husband, Nick Gosler. The grade school consisted of two rooms, each with a teacher and four grades. The teacher called the grade she wanted to work with to the front of the room. The children in that grade then sat on a row of chairs in front of her desk. If she asked you to read, you had to stand when you read.

The teacher always carried a yardstick, and if she didn't like what you were doing, she hit you on the legs. Everyone accepted this as normal back then. No parents would interfere on that score! And the parents might have been right.

In the early grades we also had a hygiene class. We had lessons on how to keep yourself clean, how to brush your teeth (there was no dental floss in those days) and what foods were good to eat. I was proud that my family knew about cleanliness. Every Saturday night, just before my bedtime, we filled a washtub full of hot water. We had a routine about who bathed first–Elsie Rene, then me, then Jim. After we were put to bed, the folks took their baths. Also we ate good foods. Basically the foods that the teachers emphasized in class were the ones we grew locally–milk, eggs and vegetables from our gardens.

This was during prohibition, so no one discussed drinking, which was illegal. But the teachers would talk about smoking and how it was bad for your health. The older men, like Grandpa, did not smoke. Instead they pulled out big plugs of tobacco, tore off a piece and chewed away. Women did not smoke; it was frowned upon. So only the younger men smoked.

Every time we had these lessons I thought with pride of my Dad, who I had never seen drink or smoke.

"My Dad does not smoke," I proudly announced during many such lessons.

One day, as I came home, Mother waited agitated on the porch. She was shaking a broomstick.

"You didn't water the chickens today!" she screamed, as she brandished the broom to hit me. I ran around the house, Mother in hot pursuit. More yells and screams, "They had no water!" Smack, smack! I crawled under a table, anything to get away from her.

Soon she tired and stopped.

We both went our separate ways.

I crawled out to check on the water. The big hen house was in good order. I had forgotten to care for a few chickens that were kept next to our porch door, or maybe their thirst and the heat had emptied the pans. As I put water in the pans, I puzzled something out. Mother usually took the easy way. Why did she beat me? Certainly it would have been easier for her to water these few chickens than to run around beating me.

During this time, and for years after, Mother used to beat me like clockwork every month. She would get her period, and I seemed to annoy her more than the other children. I learned to avoid my painful contacts with her whenever possible. I tried to stay out of the house.

One day, after Mother had finished beating me with the broom, Jim came to me tenderly and said, "You do the best you can and then you get a lickin'." I think he was making a profound statement about how he viewed life. Still, I never remember her yelling at Jim.

Our family on the Rogler homestead

But once, years later, she yelled at Elsie Rene.

After that outburst, I went into the bedroom I shared with Elsie Rene to comfort her. To my surprise, Elsie Rene was reading a book and not upset at all.

"When Mother yells," she acidly commented, "I just look at her and think how silly she looks."

So Elsie Rene taught me that nature can't be defied. Because of gravity you will always fall down, not up, at least here on earth. There are some things you just have to accept. One of those things for me to accept was Mother.

My only fight, ever, with Elsie Rene involved clothes. The three of us children always came home from school for lunch. After lunch on this particular day I changed my clothes to look my best for some special function. What it was I can't remember; from time to time we children were called upon to recite a poem or sing a song, or something of the like. I wore a lovely silk dress. It was a soft green with brown stripes. I wore silk stockings and dressy brown shoes.

To understand how special this was you need to know something about our clothing.

Most of our clothes were homemade. Our underwear was made out of flour or sugar sacks. Dress material was ordered from the Sears or Montgomery Ward catalogues. So, now you can see why the silk dress was so special. I thought I looked great!

It rained while we were eating lunch.

As we walked back to school Elsie Rene kicked mud at me. I ended up hitting her; maybe I even beat her up.

That was the only fight Elsie Rene and I ever had in our whole lives. But worse was in store for me that day.

That evening, when I returned home, Mother met me at the door. Our neighbor, Mr. Allen, had seen the incident and snitched on me. I guess he hadn't seen what Elsie Rene had done first. Mother didn't even ask me what had happened! I got a real beating that evening.

Jim and I seldom fought. But late one afternoon Jim and I were over at the barn. Frequently on rainy afternoons we would spend some time there, climbing the straight ladder to the hayloft where we could look at forbidden treasures. Mother had two large wooden chests, with rounded tops and metal straps, which she kept in the hayloft. In them she kept every important paper she ever received. The ones I most liked to read were the valentines, which struck Jim and me as extremely old-fashioned. We hooted and giggled at each other each time we read the word "love." Anyhow on this particular day, I was up in the hayloft and Jim below in the barn, when Jim started throwing corncobs up at me. Some of the corncobs hit me on the legs. I retaliated. I stepped to the edge of the hayloft opening and without looking threw a corncob down.

There was a loud cry. I dashed down. Just outside the barn, I found Jim on the ground writhing in agony. He was holding his eye.

As soon as he could control himself, he ran to the house to tell Mother.

For once, I don't remember getting punished. She was busy putting cold compresses on the eye. He had a black eye, but no other damage. Thank goodness!

He never threw corncobs at me again.

And that was the only black eye I ever gave a man.

Mother graduates from college

4
A Musical Surprise

There is something that happened one summer that I need to tell you about.

Our custom during the hot summer days was for Grandpa and Dad to return home for lunch, or rather the large mid-day meal we called "dinner." After eating they napped while the Kansas mid-day temperature rose, often higher than 100 degrees.

One day, as the men were half- napping, a truck drove up to the house. Dad got up immediately and went out. He came back into the house, put his lean and muscular arm over Mother's rounded shoulder, and walked her to the truck. I didn't know what was happening, but I saw Mother's look of delight.

Dad had surprised her with the gift of a piano.

The furniture was rearranged and the piano brought into the living room. Immediately Mother sat down on the piano stool and began playing. Until that moment, I had no idea she played the piano. I was delighted!

From then on, as I was outside playing in the evening, I'd stop and listen to her play.

Mother only played classical music, not the popular kind that you could sing to. We weren't a family that went around singing. She never told us the names of the pieces she played, and to this day I cannot tell you what they were; only that they were classical. I enjoyed them, whatever their names.

It turned out that she had studied music in college. She told me she rode sidesaddle, house to house, to give piano lessons when she was younger.

I have seen pictures of her in college. Her blonde hair piled up like a halo around her head; some wayward hairs softly straying. Light shines on her high forehead and intelligent eyes. Her dresses are tight-collared and tight waisted, but softened with pleats and lace. She was unbelievably lovely.

This opened up all sorts of possibilities to me about Mother and the life she might have had.

I might have told you this before, but Mother was educated. She went to Kansas State Teachers College in Emporia and studied journalism and music.

She had an offer to work for the *Saturday Evening Post* in Philadelphia. But by that time she had met Dad. She wanted nothing more in life than to return home and marry him. And, after a trip to Boston for a teacher's conference and New York, where she purchased the fabric for her wedding gown, she did just that. She returned and lived the life we lived.

With the arrival of the piano, Mother started Elsie Rene and me on lessons. It was a brief episode. These never followed a set schedule, were rather hit-and-miss, and neither of us ever learned to play.

Soon, however, the neighbor's children were coming for lessons. The whole area benefited from that piano. For years one of her students played at the local church services. That girl's mother did our wash in exchange for the piano lessons for her daughter. This was a blessing!

Each household task took a lot of energy in those days, and most women had set days for their chores. Monday was for washing, Tuesday for ironing. Friday was baking for the weekend.

Just imagine what you needed to do to wash the clothes! We carried water by the bucketful into the house and put it in a long copper boiler. This basin was about eighteen inches tall, three feet long, and had handles on both ends. It, in turn, was put on the wood stove to heat. While it heated Mother whittled big flakes from a block of homemade soap. She made the soap herself by saving every piece of fat and grease from her cooking in a container by the wood-burning cook stove. This she mixed with water that soaked overnight in a bucket of ashes. Cooking the mixture produced a rough yellowish soap.

White linens would then be boiled in the soapy waters. We had a "washing machine"–a lever that you pulled back and forth to churn the clothes. We then took a stick to pick up the steaming clothes and put them through a hand-cranked wringer, where they would fall into a tub of clear water to be rinsed. After, they would be wrung out again and carried to the clothesline to dry in the sun. Last, everything was ironed by hand.

I saw the piano lessons as just one example of how smart Mother was. First, she had a skill she could teach. Second, she got out of doing the laundry, which was heavy, hard work!

Doing the laundry

The South Fork River, where we would ice skate in the winter

5
The Seasons of the Year

Life was vastly different back then; it was far simpler in some respects than today. But as the laundry story shows: more work, harder. Yet still more simple.

Spring is a beautiful time in Kansas. I think it starts in March, right? Well, by that time we usually had a little light snow on the ground. The sun would start melting more snow each day. Then in the timber, I could see the grass begin to come up in muddy patches. This was a sure sign that warmth was on the way. Next, with all that melting, the prairie grass peeked through the snow in the pastures and the days would start being warmer. The sun changed. It grew stronger; you felt its warmth. The quality of the light changed, too; slowly the sunlight became less blue and more golden.

At this point the wildflowers began to appear. The first wild-flower was the dandelion—Kansas has a lot of them dotting the road-sides and adding to the warm happy feeling. When the dandelions arrived I would be so hungry for something fresh that I would run out to gather their greens. Such good eating! In a matter of days, my gath-erings would also include the greens of other plants—blue stems and docks. Every spring I gathered as many of these greens as I could find and the family enjoyed them boiled with an egg for lunch.

Mother was the one who taught me how to do this. The first few springs after we moved to the Rogler place, as soon as the grass ap-peared in the timber, she would walk out to the edge of the timber with me, one of us carrying our little metal pail.

As we crouched on our knees to look at the thin yellow-green shoots, she pointed to one or another little blade and said, "This is good to eat, this is good to eat, and this is good to eat." Each identified leaf went into the little pail. And so I learned about the edible plants. I guess she learned this from her mother or father, and they from the Indians. But this is just my supposition.

Later in the spring, other wild flowers, like wild lilies, burst into colorful bloom. But what I remember the most is our orchard. What a joy to see all those fruit trees burst into bloom! Finally the lilacs and roses around the house started to bloom, and then the flowers we planted around the house. In spring the place really was quite beautiful. By Decoration Day there were armloads of flowers to be cut and gathered. On that day we put flowers on the graves of all the Roglers, anyone that belonged to us we would put flowers on.

Spring was also a sign that Dad would come home for Easter. His quiet presence made my life easier. He always did little things to please me when he came home. I believed in the Easter bunny, with a passion. Each Easter I made grass nests in the yard. Dad would put candy eggs in them now and then during the day. This made Easter my favorite holiday; Dad and the Easter Bunny were paying attention to me. One Easter, when I was five or so, Mother watched as Dad filled my nests with eggs several times during the day. She must have noted my childish delight in finding the eggs. Dad finished filling the nests and went into the house, leaving me still hard at work finding my treats.

I looked up as Mother left the house to tell me something.

"I am glad to see you are enjoying yourself," she said flatly. Then, adding as she warmed to her theme, "but you're old enough now to know something."

I was entranced and wondered what grown-up secret she was going to share with me. It was very unusual for her to make a trip outside; she rarely went out at all. And we were not close. So, I knew this was going to be important.

"There is no Easter Bunny."

I cried. I insisted that there was. Just think of all the eggs the Easter Bunny had left me!

Mother did not argue. She turned and walked back into the house. A little joy went out of my life.

Looking back now, I think she resented it when Dad did anything for me. Dad and I had a good relationship. Well, I still grew up but my childhood could have been better.

Spring was also the time when we took our shoes off, because, of course, when we were young we went barefoot. We only wore shoes to school and Sunday school in the warm months. When I first took my winter shoes off, I could feel every stone on my feet. But somehow I knew that my soles would get tough. If I just bore it, the calluses would grow and then I would not feel the pain. I learned this as a lesson for life.

Another great thing happened each spring. As the days grew warmer Grandpa Rogler's place became the "Disneyland" of Matfield. I never had a girl friend. My friends were the fellows who came down to see Jim, and as the days grew longer they came in droves. Elsie Rene stayed inside reading with Mother. I wanted to keep my distance from Mother. Instead, I played outside with Jim and the local boys.

In spring we played baseball. I insisted I had to be the pitcher. And so I was.

Jim and I taught ourselves to ride one spring. Grandpa had

Local boys prepare to play ball

Local boys riding

two gray mares. He used them both for farm work and to ride. When he rode, Grandpa used a saddle. He had only one saddle. Jim and I learned to ride these horses bareback. We took a bridle out to the pasture and put it on the horse. Next, we led the horse to something we could climb upon to get on the horse's back.

One day Mother saw us using our typical process to mount. Wonder of wonders, she actually came out of the house. Mother rarely came outside. She was frowning.

"That is not the way to get on a horse's back," she said. "You put your hands on the back, give a jump and swing your right leg over the back."

I thought, "Mother knows this?"

"Here let me show you," she added.

She took the bridle in her hand. She put her hands on the horse's back. She jumped. Her feet went up a few inches. She was fat and out of shape.

There was a moment of silence.

Mother handed the horse's bridle back to Jim and said, "Well, all right, get on as you were doing."

We did.

We learned that horses had personalities. The horse that Jim rode always had to be in front. Or maybe my horse just could not stand to be in front. In any event, I could never win a race. I learned this the

Mother in her bathing suit, 1905

hard way. One day I was in front. My horse hunkered her head down, pounded the ground with her two front feet and stopped. I flew over her head and landed on a rock. I limped to the house and never tried to win another race.

Another thing about Kansas: during the summer there was only a thin veneer between Kansas and Hell.

Temperatures frequently reached 100 degrees or higher.

Still there were aspects of the summer that were wonderful.

On the hot summer days, all the local children gathered at Grandpa's place by a large deep area in the South Fork River. Everyone called it the "Round Hole." It was the perfect spot for swimming, deep and cool, free of the leeches that were found in many other locations, and shaded by trees. One of the trees had a rope "swing" with a knot in it for diving. In the morning only boys were allowed to swim. They skinny-dipped. In the afternoon girls could join them. By that time everyone was in bathing suits that covered much of our bodies, and my mother would supervise. Oh, the fun!

Also, during the summer Dad came home to farm. It was so

Dad on tractor, 1940s

good to have him with us morning and night. He would get up early and fix breakfast. For himself he usually went out into the garden, picked the nicest ripe tomato, sliced it, and doused it with a heavy coating of sugar. Sometimes he made this for me as well. Dad always did little nice things for other people, as opposed to asking you to do things for him.

To make more money he bought a tractor that he hired out to other farmers during the day. It was so much easier for the men than using a horse to plow the fields. At night, Dad used the tractor himself, operating with the tractor lights to tend his fields. That one tractor planted many acres. We didn't know it then, but this was the beginning of a major change in farm life. Before the tractor, a family could only care for 160 acres or so, even with the help of many sons. With the development of tractors and other machinery, farmers could handle thousands of acres of land.

Today they even have tractors that almost drive themselves by way of satellites. So I have read!

During the summer in the hot afternoons, Jim spent time digging earthworms for fish bait. One summer day I looked down while Jim and I were playing ball and said, "Oh, look at that big worm!"

It was almost twelve inches long. We were amazed at its size. Jim got a hatchet to cut it up. Later that evening, when Dad came home from working in the fields, we ran with excitement to tell him about the big worm. Curious, he walked over and looked down.

"That's not a worm," he calmly said, "It's a baby rattlesnake."

Without more ado, he walked into the house.

When Jim did find worms we went fishing. Our little poles were made from tree limbs with string tied at one end. At the other end of the string we placed a small sinker and a small fishhook.

Then we walked to the South Fork River that flowed through Grandpa's farm to a place called the "flat rocks." We scrambled down a slippery dirt slope, stopping on flat limestone rocks near a small waterfall–maybe two to three feet high. As we sat on the rocks, we put a worm on the hook, put the fishhook in the water, and waited for a small sunfish to bite. Often we could see the fish shimmering in the water, dragonflies and water skimmers hovering just above. Any fish we caught was tossed into a pail of water.

In the evening Dad went down to the South Fork and, using the sunfish as bait, he set lines to catch bigger fish overnight. We checked these lines bright and early the next morning. A catch meant fresh fish to eat that day! There were bass, catfish, and eel. Delicious!

On the Fourth of July our custom was to kill the first spring chicken and to have the first fresh corn on the cob. Then, everything was topped off with ice cream. It was always a great dinner! In the evening Dad set off fireworks. This was a day we enjoyed.

Another annual event occurred every summer. Mother's sister and her husband Uncle Whit, daughter Virginia, and son Junior would visit us for a week.

I always loved it when they came. Virginia and I would go

Virginia

down to the shallow part of the river and gather flower petals. We would sing and dance like water sprites, and scatter petals in the flowing water.

Aside from this, Jim and Virginia usually played together, because they were the same age. Junior and I palled out; usually outside doing something that we thought was fun, maybe swinging or catching fireflies in the evening. It was good to have someone else to play with.

One year, when it was time for them to go, Junior didn't want to leave.

As he pouted and cried, Mother said he could stay with us. That impressed me.

The family gathered around to say our goodbyes. Uncle Whit, Aunt Elsie, and Virginia bundled into the car. Junior stayed on the grass with us.

Junior pelted the car with rocks as they drove away. Then, when they had gone less than a hundred yards, he started crying!

Uncle Whit backed up the car and Junior happily jumped in. His clothes were already packed in it. They understood him so well!

Of course in the summer, during August, we celebrated my birthday on August 8 and Jim's on August 2. For birthdays Mother made a cake. We could have any kind of cake we wanted—so long as it was angel food. Mother made great angel food cakes, beating by hand 8 egg whites till they were stiff and frothy and then hand folding in the flour and other ingredients.

During the fall, we were busy harvesting. What was done–and when it occurred–depended on the crop. Our two main fall crops were corn and silage from kafir corn–a long stock with loosely packed seed heads that came from Africa. We used the corn, as well as the silage, to feed our livestock. The corn was harvested in late September or early October when the kernels were matured and hard.

Dad hated harvesting corn, and grew only as much as we needed for our own use. The men walked along the rows wearing heavy gloves and wielding a metal hook. They husked the ear of all leaves using the metal hook, ripped the now-naked ear from the stalk and threw it into a horse-drawn wagon. It was a rough job, but one that had to be done. Then we placed the ears of corn in our barn to be used as needed throughout the winter, for our cattle and my "beloved" chickens!

Harvesting the silage was also tiring work. Dad farmed quite a bit of silage and its harvest required the help of neighbors. Seven or eight people needed to pitch in to get this done. For one thing, the silage needed to be harvested at just the right time—when the water content was neither too high nor too low, so that the animals would get the maximum nutrients over the winter. This meant that someone ran a machine that chomped the stocks and heads into small pieces, others ran trucks to move the silage from our far-off fields into our silos, and Dad of course directed it all.

Never one for the house, when I was old enough, I also helped driving a truck full of silage to and from our silo. I was content to do any work, even men's work, which took me away from the house and my painful contacts with Mother. Long before it was fashionable, I spent my days in blue jeans and overalls, working along with the men.

Also in the fall, usually after the first rain in September, we planted our wheat crop. This crop would be harvested in June. But prior to that, from October to January, it provided a winter pasture for our cattle. In January the cattle were pulled off, so that the spring crop of wheat would grow.

On fall days when farming work was light, all the town boys came to play with Jim. Not having any girl friend, I again joined in—playing football with the boys, but this time doing as I was told during the games. The high school also played football games against the other area high schools. The quality varied greatly, but the whole village turned out for these games—the men and women and the lower grades kids. They would discuss the plays in detail over the following week. Finally, every fall there was a county fair in Cottonwood Falls—with a show of local produce and the judging of 4H projects. There also was a Ferris wheel and merry–go-round. A welcome break in our heavy routine!

In the fall we often had taffy pull parties with other children from the local school. One of the mothers, but not my Mother, would let it be known that she planned to make taffy one weekend night. She cooked the taffy in a big pot and when it was the right consistency spread it out onto a large buttered pan. Divided into sections as it cooled, the children paired off to pull and twist the sugary mass. As we did, it changed from clear to creamy and began to firm up. Then we cut it into small pieces and ate to our heart's content.

So you see our lives were simple. I didn't travel much in those days, like we do today. A trip of a few miles was planned for. There were no movie theatres. Basically our entertainment was at our homes, with friends and in our little local village.

In the winters, which were terribly cold and bitter, we ice skated on the river. Sometimes the boys built bonfires to toast marshmallows and keep warm. The fires would roar and send off sparks as we thrust our hands closer, and turned away our over-hot faces. Sometimes itinerant players would come to put on a show in the local school auditorium. There was nothing distinguished about these shows, except they were someplace to go. It was always good for a change in the dreary days of winter. Also, there was sledding on a little hill not too far from Great-Aunt Adaline's house. I wore long mid-calf woolen skirts in the winter and sometimes they froze to my sled. This happened one time when a neighbor boy made a chain of 3 or 4 sleds and attached them to a horse for a ride along the road. Oh that was fun!

On a more practical level, winter was the time for harvesting ice. Matfield had an icehouse.

When the South Fork froze over and the ice was thick enough, the men would saw the ice in blocks, haul it to the icehouse, and pack it in sawdust. If the ice didn't hold through the summer, folks would drive to Cottonwood and buy chunks of ice. There was an icemaker and a large central icehouse in Cottonwood.

Also in the winter we butchered our animals, so we had great beef and mincemeat for pies. During the winter we packed our hogs, which were freshly slaughtered, in salt to keep them over the summer. Beef was canned, if it was unlikely to be consumed during the winter. We made fruit cakes and candy. We ate canned fruits and vegetables, and stored root vegetables too–potatoes and turnips.

We really had good food with very little out-of-pocket cost; just plenty of hard work. Much later, in the 1930s, a central freezer opened in Cottonwood Falls. What a convenience! You rented a drawer in the central freezer and then, when you butchered your stock, they would cut, wrap, and store it for you. We marveled at this modern convenience.

It was amazing how self-sufficient our little village was—whether it was the things we ate, entertainment, and even in matters of religion. We did it ourselves.

The highlight of winter was Christmas—a low-key holiday by today's standards.

Every year the school put on a Christmas program in the auditorium. A live tree was decorated with strings of popcorn and cranberries. Every child had a part in the program. Jim and I usually sang in a group with the other children.

After the program, Santa arrived in costume and handed out gifts. Families brought gifts for their children. One year I got a string of "pearl" beads. I remember it to this day, as a delightful surprise.

We loved the evening. When it was over, we would walk home in the cold snowy night. When the moon shone, the outdoors was a beautiful world.

At home we did not make much of Christmas. However, the folks would always kill a steer just before Christmas. Dad would feed this steer special, just for home use. He selected the steer when it was a calf, in the spring. Then to make it fatten fast he fed it special with grain in addition to our good prairie grass. A few days before Christmas, a couple of Dad's friends would come over and together they would butcher the special steer.

First, Dad took it near a tree and then grabbed his gun from the house and shot the steer in the head. Quickly after this, Dad slit the steer's throat and, using a pulley, hung it head down from the tree. This was to get the blood out. If you don't get the blood out of the body all the meat parts have a lot of blood in them and the meat will deteriorate faster.

Grandpa told me one Christmas, as we watched this production, that in the olden days the men drank the warm blood; but, when I was growing up, we did not use the blood. At the most, we sometimes collected it to give to the pigs. While the blood was draining, the men pulled the steer's hide off, gutted it and quartered it. The meat quarters were hung in the barn, where—in our cold winters—the meat would stay frozen till spring. From time to time during the winter Dad cut pieces of meat for our use.

Then Mother's work began. She made a heavy broth by boiling the skull of the animal, with flavor coming from all the meat and marrow it contained. Stripping the meat off the bone, she added raisins and apples and seasoning according to her recipe. All that was boiled again, and canned to use later on in pies and puddings.

Christmas day we always had suet pudding stuffed with raisins, prunes, and currents; a very tasty dish. Otherwise, it just wasn't that significant a holiday at our place. But as we got older, at my request, we cut down branches of cedar trees and decorated them.

There is one Christmas I will never forget. In the winter of 1924, we lived with Dad for a few months as he drilled for oil in Eldorado, about thirty miles south. During the time we were away, Great-Aunt Adaline took care of Grandpa.

Dad must have felt that his prospects looked good. President Calvin Coolidge had encouraged the growth of business and with this growth, mining boomed. The mining must have put some spare change in Dad's pockets.

I was nine that Christmas. Dad bought me my only toy ever—a beautiful doll. I remember her. She was made of white kid leather that was soft and creamy to the touch. She had real hair and eyes that opened and shut. I was thrilled!

Later in the afternoon I left her on a chair while Dad took the family for a ride in the car.

When we returned home, she was on the floor, her hair pulled off her head. Somehow, Jeff, our dog, got into the house and chewed off her wig. My throat tightened. Could I fix the wig?

Before I could do anything, Mother moved in. She picked up the doll and threw her in the garbage. I never saw that doll again.

She was the only doll I ever had.

I would love to have that doll today.

The Rogler Family

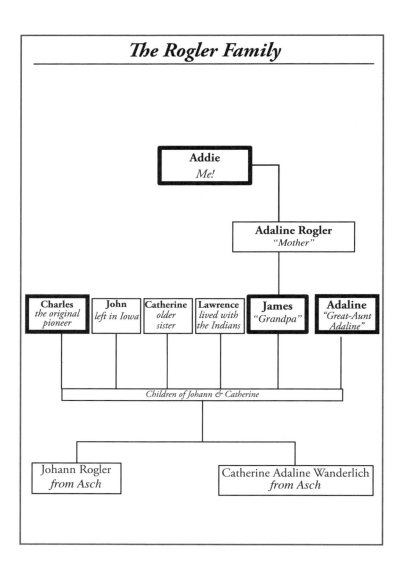

Addie
Me!

Adaline Rogler
"Mother"

| **Charles** the original pioneer | **John** left in Iowa | **Catherine** older sister | **Lawrence** lived with the Indians | **James** *"Grandpa"* | **Adaline** *"Great-Aunt Adaline"* |

Children of Johann & Catherine

Johann Rogler
from Asch

Catherine Adaline Wanderlich
from Asch

6
Grandpa Rogler

When Dad was away, as he often was, trying to make a better living for us, Grandpa Rogler was a calming presence. I think I was Grandpa Rogler's favorite grandchild. Every now and then he'd silently give me a peppermint from a bag he kept beside his wall clock–high on a shelf in our living room. I was the only one he gave peppermints to. As he did this, and every time I got up close to Grandpa, I could catch the whiff of his chewing tobacco on his breath.

To my annoyance, he had his own special nickname for me, "Dovy." As always I wanted to be called Adaline; but when I complained to Mother she explained that Dovy was a very affectionate name that meant "Dove." Thinking of the peppermints, and all the affection, I never complained to Grandpa about the name.

Also, when the weather started to get warm in the spring, I was the only one Grandpa let take out the hair clippers and clip off all his hair. After my clipping, he was a "bald man" for the warm months. As the weather started to cool, he let his hair grow. By spring, he had beautiful gray curls at his neckline. I loved the way they looked.

As Grandpa and I walked about doing chores on our land, we watched for Indian arrowheads. I'm sorry that I didn't take better care of our finds. One of Grandpa's fields–the cornfield closest to the house—was particularly fruitful. There were all sorts of arrows, knives, scrappers, and tomahawk heads. Many were just lying on top of the ground. Until the 1930s, when the land was terraced as part of a government program to control rainfall and increase crop production, you would find flint chips in a circle where the Indians sat around fires and worked to make tools. Grandpa Rogler said the field had once been an Indian campground. We called this area the "Indian Field."

Most of my elders seemed a little fearful of the Indians. My grandfather's brother Charles even enlisted in 1864 as a private in Company C, 17th Kansas Volunteers, to protect citizens from Indian attacks. But he served only for 100 days. Also, there was an oft-repeated family story of how, whenever Indians were in the South Fork area, the Roglers put their baby, my great-aunt Adaline, in a rotted-out tree stump to hide her. They were afraid she would be stolen. So you can see that people at that time did not look kindly on Indians. They certainly did not socialize with them.

Through the conversations with Grandpa I came to understand that Grandpa Rogler had a different perspective about the Indians than others in our area. He viewed them with deep respect.

Although there were no Indians in Matfield when I was growing up, Grandpa told me there were some Indians buried on the hills east of his land. They were buried facing the rising sun. He also told me that his oldest sister, Catherine Rogler Yaeger, walking by herself in those frontier days long ago came upon an Indian squaw burying her child. The women looked at each other with sympathy. Touched, Grandpa said that Catherine waited for the squaw to leave and erected a headstone to mark the grave.

According to Grandpa, the Indians used to come by the house in the earlier days of the 1860s, a few at a time, mostly looking for food. Unlike other settlers, he always gave them something. Although his folks were afraid the Indians might hurt them, Grandpa said this was never the case. In fact, if anything, the Indians imparted valuable information to the Roglers when they first settled on the land. They told the Roglers how to plant corn. As we chatted, he described it to me.

"With a stick, you make a hole; you place a few corn kernels there and a small fish, and then cover everything up. That was what both the Indians and we did."

Also, Grandpa Rogler said the Indians told him exactly where to build his house, in an area that never flooded. I heard the story, felt a little safer in the thought of the wisdom of my elders, and thought not much more of it.

I never questioned why Grandpa Rogler's views of the Indians seemed to differ so much from those of others in our family, or why the Indians helped him so. Never thought to ask why. Only recently I heard for the first time that as a young boy Grandpa Rogler ran away to live with the Indians for two years. When I first heard this I was shocked. He never spoke of this to me, and we were close. I wondered if it was true. He was the least adventuresome person I ever knew. No motivation. But he was sociable. Now, it turns out, many branches of the family, but not his own, were aware of this period in his life. He and his brother Lawrence lived with the Indians for two years, learned their sign language and served as interpreters between the settlers and the Indians. Perhaps, given the prejudices of the day, it was something he was ashamed of. Guess he couldn't expect that 90 years later, his children and grandchildren would love to know about his adventures during this period. And that we might view it as one of the most interesting, admirable parts of his life.

Another of the special things Grandpa and I would do together is milk the cow he kept in a shed on the other side of our valley. When I was nine, he taught me how to milk her as well. As far as I know, milking cows was "men's work" and I was the only girl in our valley that did this.

Today, for sanitary reasons, dairy folk wash and clean the cows before they take the milk. But we just went right out there and started milking. Grandpa taught me to put my hands on the teats and, starting at the top, to squeeze my fingers shut one finger at a time. I was so pleased that I could do this. In the winter we left the milk outside our back door, but in the summer I took it down to the spring in our metal pail and placed it where the water was always cool. The next day, after the milk had cooled, Grandpa and I usually skimmed off the cream and made butter with a wooden churn or hand mixer.

Nearly every Sunday, we made ice cream. Jim and I took turns hand cranking the wooden freezer. If we had extra milk, which was frequently the case without refrigeration, Mother mostly fed the excess to the pigs. Sometimes, however, she let the milk become sour, then simmered it on the back of the stove for a short time. Draining off the whey, we would be left with cottage cheese.

Milk tasted different then–not like it does today. Today our milk is homogenized, pasteurized, vitamins are added.

When I was a child, milk's flavors varied with the time of year.

In the spring, our cow ate wild onions that sprouted earlier in the season than the grass. I could taste those wild onions in the milk. That was the one time of year I didn't like the taste.

Grandpa Rogler's birthday was February 28. One year on his birthday I asked him if he was rich. He said no, he wished he had spent his earlier years differently. He was the youngest son in his family. Unlike the other Roglers, he had not been ambitious and loved to loaf in the village. He seemed truly sad about this. Maybe he viewed the time as an Indian interpreter as wasted, too. He spoke of the loafing, but not of running off.

Years later, when I grew up, I learned there was more to be sad about. Mother told me. Many times as a young girl she stood by the window waiting for her father to come home, worrying that he would return well lubricated with alcohol. His drunken fits were frequently recorded by the townsfolk, and even his own nephews, in a "good-humored" prank, placed at least one account in the local press. Mother was little and afraid for him. The feeling of insecurity lasted her whole life–she worried about everything. I think this was part of the reason she was afraid to leave the Flint Hills. I guess we all have our crosses to bear.

Mother also told me why Grandpa stopped heavy drinking. He got some bad liquor and one day came home blind. I don't know when this was or how long the blindness lasted.

As Mother told me this story, I thought of Grandma Rogler's Women's Christian Temperance Union pin. No wonder Grandma wore it so visibly.

Even when we lived with him, however, Grandpa continued to drink a homemade elderberry wine. Every fall, as the wild elderberries ripened on the farm, Grandpa gathered them to make his wine. I would tag along to help gather the berries. I never saw him drink the liquor. But I knew that he kept the wine in a stoneware jug down in the storm cellar. Often in the afternoons he would slip downstairs for a "nip" of the dark blue liquid. He kept a tin cup nearby to use for this purpose. This was the only liquor allowed in the house when I was growing up–and Grandpa was the only one who imbibed. Jim and I might have snuck a sip, but we never did; Grandpa told us that he frequently got the runs from the stuff.

On the days when he was home, my father never went to the village in the afternoons. Instead he spent the time at work on his fields. But Grandpa Rogler never broke his habit of going to the village. Every afternoon Grandpa went to Snedegar's—the local post office and grocery store in Matfield. There, with some other men from the town, he spent summer time sitting outside on the benches, and winter days by the potbellied stove, spitting his chewing tobacco into the spittoon and gossiping. He brought a lot of the gossip home.

As I grew older, Mother and I worked around the house, cooking or the like. She shared the gossip with me, as well as stories about her family. There was always a lot of gossip in the community and Mother–through Grandpa–was a major transmitter of it. I don't remember the gossip after all these years. Of course, everyone knew a lot about everyone else and their parents and maybe even their grandparents; still, I think much of the talk was about the small daily occurrences of life, things like who is sick and who is planting what crops. Crops and weather were big topics of conversations. As far as I was aware the town lacked most exciting events, like murders or robberies, that you hear so much about on a daily basis today. Even unmarried girls and pregnancies, I didn't hear about, if we had any. Of course, we didn't have a great number of young girls either.

Part 2
My Family

Rogler ranch Easter picnic 1913 (Mother with baby Jim in back)

7
The Rogler Family Story

Many times when I spoke with Mother or Grandpa or Great-Aunt Adaline, I was told the story of how the Rogler family came to Kansas. The Roglers loved to tell the story.

My great-grandparents were Johann Rogler, born February 16, 1808, and Catherine Adaline Wunderlich, born February 1, 1814. Both came from the town of Asch in western Bohemia, a predominantly German region that eventually became part of the Austrian Empire. They were married there in 1830 and in the years that followed had four boys, including my grandfather, and two daughters, including my great-aunt Adaline, whose name may have been spelled Adeline in Europe. Spellings seem to have been more phonetic and less rigid in those days.

During the time just before our Civil War, Europeans frequently heard about the new, vital republic across the Atlantic. Families who wanted land, food, and freedom dreamed of America. In this they were aided by various pamphlets—basically, the 19th century form of advertising for new housing lots in America. An added appeal was the absence of compulsory military service. This seems to have been the main motivation for the Roglers. I was always told that Johann and Catherine dreamed of living in a peaceful country where their sons would not have to go to war.

In 1852, Johann sold much of his property and gave the money to Charles, his sixteen-year-old son.* Johann used the money to send Charles to the United States to find a new home for the family. The family did not hear from him for years and assumed he was dead.

---

*According to some accounts Charles was thirteen when he left Asch; others said that he left home at seventeen or at twenty-one. My account mostly reflects my recollections of what the pioneer generation told me, but I have changed Charles' departure date to 1852 because the rest of the story seems to require a longer sojourn in America.

Meanwhile, Charles initially settled in the Western Reserve country of northern Ohio (according to his son Henry). He may have worked in Sandusky, Ohio, where he skinned cattle in a tannery for the first three or four years. After a while, he made his way to Iowa, which was at that time the staging ground between the eastern United States and the high prairie grasses of the western plains. Iowa, acquired by the United States along with Kansas as part of the Louisiana Purchase in 1803, had only just recently become the twenty-ninth state, in 1846. As the crisis that led to the Civil War deepened, there was a great interest in populating the West with "free" or "slave" states. In 1854 Stephen Douglas proposed the Kansas-Nebraska Bill to enable the settlement of the West, although his main interest was in building a transcontinental railroad. Violent fights erupted between those who wanted Kansas to be free and their pro-slavery opponents, and the state became known as "Bleeding Kansas."

Possibly while working as a farm hand, Charles became friends with Henry Brandley. In 1859 he and Brandley set out on foot from Council Bluffs, Iowa, to find their fortune in the Kansas Territory.

Folk legend has it that they walked the whole way. They worked for a short while in a brickyard in Tecumseh, six miles east of Topeka, and then joined a small group of home seekers that pushed on as far as Cottonwood Falls. Very possibly on April 1, 1859, Charles and Henry walked into Chase County, Kansas, together. There were two cabins in Cottonwood Falls in 1859. Learning that the most choice parcels had already been taken, they purchased land near the South Fork River from some earlier settlers who wanted to leave.

At this point, Charles decided– for some reason–to write home to Germany. The letter arrived in Asch, which at that time was a town of about 8,000 and had been inhabited by Germans since the eleventh century. The townspeople had professions and areas of specialization. Homes were built of stone, to last hundreds of years. There were family and friends connected by diverse ties and relationships that spanned many generations. History and customs governed one's daily life.

Johann was a woodworker, a refined craftsman, and, no doubt, a guild member. He had farm land just three miles outside of town and walked each morning to a studio in town from which he plied his wares.

In 1859, after years of silence, Johann and Catherine received the letter from Charles telling them to meet him in Council Bluffs Iowa. With great excitement, Johann and Catherine sold their worldly possessions. This allowed Johann Rogler to bring $1,000 in gold with him, a considerable sum of money. It was the equivalent of more than $1.7 million in today's money.

Leaving loved ones behind; the family boarded a large sailing ship in Hamburg that was bound for New Orleans. The voyage took fourteen weeks, far longer than the normal trip which I think in those days usually lasted only three or so weeks. Even a planned trip that long would be difficult! Grandpa, who was a small boy during the voyage, told me the ocean was rough, the ship was dirty, and they were seasick. They must have dreamed of land, and starting their new life. Did they try to imagine what the future held? Did they envision vast tracts of fertile land and peaceful valleys? I can only guess, there is no record.

Covered wagons, Manhattan, Kansas, 1860

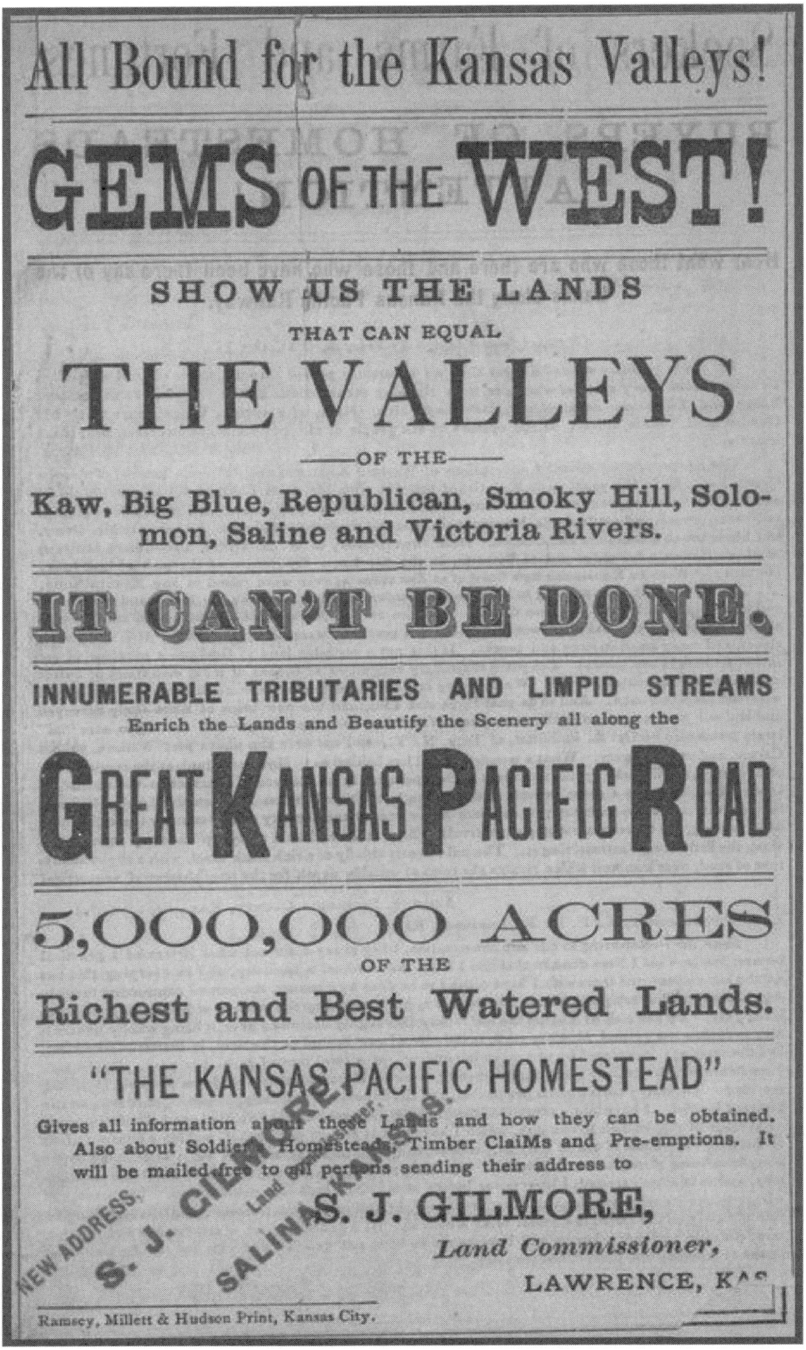

Brochure advertising land between 1870 and 1880

WHY INVEST IN KANSAS PACIFIC
LANDS?

Because you have the vast expanse of 5,000,000 Acres to select from, with every variety of Land, Bottom and Upland, Undulating Valley, and Rolling Prairie.

Because the PURITY of the CLIMATE is UNSURPASSED—long Summers, short Winters, and genial skies.

Because the fertility of the soil *can't be beaten.* Where else can be found a soil of such rich, dark loam, varying from 3 to 15 feet in depth?

Because in proof of this, the unprecedented Crops proclaim Kansas to be the *Banner Wheat and Corn State of the Union.*

Because its Rivers, Streams and Creeks abound in every County along the Road.

Because Springs of purest water are to be found in every section.

Because of the vastness of its water power for manufacturing purposes.

Because for Stock Raising and Wool Growing, the nutritious character of its wide grassy ranges has been proved invaluable.

Because all the Lands are within an easy distance of the Great Iron Thoroughfare of the West.

Because Towns and Cities are rapidly springing up all along its entire length, with all their attendant advantages.

Because wherever a setttlement is formed, the moral and religious well being of its inhabitants are duly cared for.

Last but not least.

Because the Prices are *very low.*

Because the Terms of Credit are long, easy, liberal, and within the reach of all.

Because if you buy 160 Acres, your ride out to seek Lands will be free.

WHEN TO COME? AT ONCE!

The Company are more desirous to get their Lands settled up and improved, thereby increasing the business of its Railroad, than they are to hold them with the view of realizing higher prices, the prosperity of the settlers being the prosperity of the Railroad.

Brochure advertising land between 1870 and 1880

87

From New Orleans they took a boat up the Mississippi to Iowa where Charles met them. In Iowa they bought and provisioned a covered wagon and with Charles joined a wagon train to Kansas. Among the items they brought with them was a huge chest of flour and many homemade linens and blankets from Asch. However, coming from a settled and established country, they carried no guns.

"Can you believe that, Dovy?" Grandpa used to tell me. "We were so unprepared. We had no idea what to expect out here, we didn't even buy a gun." I would shake my head in disbelief alongside him. We always had guns in our home, and I could not imagine a life without them.

The family told the story of the trip, and of the guns. Less, however, was said about another thing, perhaps made even more amazing in its silence. Johann and Catherine left their second oldest son, John, in Iowa. I heard little about this as a child. Only that a "prosperous" family in Iowa, who had no children, wanted him badly; so John was left there. John spent the rest of his life in Iowa, raising pigs, I believe. He married and had two sons and, despite it all, he kept in touch with the rest of his family. Years later I heard that possibly John was left as an "indentured" servant to pay for debts incurred by Charles. Who will ever know the truth? The relative silence on this score, in a gossipy family, does raise a question in my mind, I must say. Did Catherine miss him? Did her heart ache?

There may have been little time to focus on these things. Maybe she came in time to believe that John was blessed.

The Roglers arrived in Kansas during one of the worst droughts in recorded history. The date is a bit fuzzy. Some family members, Mother included, said it was in 1859, but others thought it was the spring of 1860. The year 1860 is recorded in history books as the "Kansas famine." No rain sufficient for crops fell from June 1859 to November 1860. Cattle survived until the fall of 1859 on the limited prairie grass. But then wells and springs dried up, and the dusty brown wasteland grew.

Great-Aunt Adaline told me that during the journey west their wagon train often proceeded along the dried-up riverbeds, a frontier "highway to hell." This "highway" was taking them right into the heart of the drought. As they were arriving, bedraggled and bitter settlers were heading in the opposite direction, returning to the more hospitable "States." Others were too poor, or too weak, to even attempt to return. Only about a third of the population in Kansas were sufficiently provisioned to withstand the famine: they could not assist the others. They were fighting to live themselves.

By November 1860 the *Emporia News* reported that, with the exception of a few wealthy settlers, the population of Chase County did not have provisions to last one-month, and that flour, cornmeal, and meal could not be had. Worse, many settlers had lost their last cow to Spanish Fever. The Cottonwood Falls elders sent requests for aid back East noting that they were "without bread and . . . means of procuring it."

These tough settlers asked only for "a loan," and remained "confident" that they would repay it. Later that year assistance from the East was forthcoming and a greater disaster was averted.

When the Roglers arrived there were thirty-five households in the whole of the South Fork Valley, two households in Cottonwood Falls and six in Bazaar. Not one household had flour. So the Roglers shared their chest of flour with all. This provided sustenance to tide the hungry families over till assistance arrived.

These were the conditions that welcomed the Rogler family to the South Fork of the Cottonwood River in the Flint Hills of Kansas. Determined to make a go of it, and probably emotionally unable to contemplate a return, the family bought out some returning homesteaders at the fork of the Crocker and South Fork Rivers. This was near the village of Matfield Green, named in 1858 by David Mercer after two hamlets near his English home–Five Oaks Green and Matfield*.

One day, as Grandpa and I made our rounds of the farm, I commented about the number of grasshoppers.

"This is nothing," he told me. "In our early years we had a lot of locusts around." (He called the grasshoppers locusts. He may have been referring to the grasshopper infestation of 1874.)

* Joseph V. Hickey, *Ghost Settlements on the Prairie: a Biography of Thurman, Kansas*, p. 59.

Original log cabin 1859

"They came out of the sky like a cloud and obliterated the sun. They ate everything; our whole garden. They even ate the wooden fence posts. The ground was bare when they left."

During this period another threat loomed. Indians had been uprooted from their lands, promised this territory, and now were facing further dislocations. Indian uprisings in the 1860s were frequent, and the folks in near-by Bazaar used their schoolhouse as a place of refuge from Indian attacks.

In 1861 Kansas became a state. But in this time of strife and hardship, nothing was easy for Kansas and its settlers. There was much contention about whether Kansas should be a free or a slave state. Missouri, next door, was a slave state, and many people did not want to see Kansas a free one. Residents near the Kansas-Missouri border were burned and killed. The violence was high. The Roglers needed to pass through this area during their trip to Kansas from Iowa, although there are no family stories about this that I know. I understand that the Roglers sympathized with the Union. Rebel forces may have threatened Charles. At least on one occasion he was taken to the hills for questioning but subsequently released.

Is it any surprise that shortly after arriving, Charles was willing to throw in the towel? He put up a shingle offering to sell his farm for $300.

There were no takers.

The Roglers had left all to find a new and better life in America. It did not await them. But almost against their will, they and the other pioneers helped to create one.

And so the family stayed and became known and celebrated as one of the pioneer families. And, with the passage of time, the stories of those days were told and retold. And the times themselves became less fearsome, but more like a test of endurance and the human spirit.

They were a family that stayed!

They had passed the test.

Even as time passed, however, life continued to be hard.

For the Roglers, as for most pioneers, their first home was a log cabin made from trees growing nearby; floors were of dirt. (For those pioneers who made their way to western Kansas, where no trees grew, the first home was built from the Kansas sod.)

Grandpa, Lawrence, Adaline, Kate, and John the Iowa farmer
(Taken in 1888, possibly at Charles' funeral)

Water was carried into the house, and out—as were the residue of bodily functions, unless they were done outside. Bathing was in the river during summer, and during winter a sponge bath. Body odor was accepted as normal.

Clothes were made and washed by hand. They were laid over a bush to dry, or hung on a line if some rope was available. There were no sewing machines. No refrigerators.

Light came from homemade candles. Most people went to bed early.

Food was raised, or found. Rabbit, squirrel, and raccoons were caught and killed. Fish were hooked. People gathered weeds and hoped they were edible.

They came to a land where there was no fence to hold the cattle. Barbed wire wasn't invented until about 1880. Grandpa told me that his mother, Catherine, worried endlessly about the cattle and ran miles every day looking after them. She was always fearful that the cattle would wander off or be stolen.

The weather was extreme, unpredictable, and violent. There were snows and droughts and grasshopper plagues.

This was the land for which the Roglers had sold all their worldly possessions and undertaken a dangerous journey.

Johann, a furniture maker in Germany, cut down black walnut trees and made simple chairs, tables, and shelves for his family. Why he didn't go to New York or Boston or Philadelphia, I will never know. He must have known very little about the U.S. His health was poor in Kansas, but I was never told why. I keep this tough life in mind as I read excerpts of a letter he received from his brother-in-law in Germany.

Schildern, on 1 July 1872

My dear brother-in-law, sister and godfather,

   We wish that you will receive our letter and will be in best health. We are still healthy and are well.

   Dear brother-in-law, we have received your last letter and we have given it to Johann Krigner in Nassengrub since he was wondering that you are still alive so he can show your letter to his neighbours. He let us send his regards. I have sent my quick response but obviously the address was missing so you did not receive it. Dear brother-in-law, you wrote that the working . . . it is quite a lot. Here by us the carpenter receives 1-½ florins daily and also the mason, the day labourer daily 1 florin. The servant hundred and thirty kreutzer, it makes 60 k. but the people are not available because they are working in the factories with machines that are set to work. Around Asch you would find many machines. You would not know a thing in Asch if you would come back again. On the forest hill now it is built a school with a teacher.

   The Gassman has built a steam weaving factory where many people earn their money; the other Gassman [has built] a brick factory, in which they produce 5000 to 6000 bricks daily . . .

   Brother-in-law, I have to wonder that your winter corn is not very good. Our winter corn is very thin and long but the summer corn is standing very good. The harvest will begin in 14 days when the weather is dry. The corn prices are middle.

   Dear brother-in-law, your godchild wanted to write to you but I thought I have to write so you can see that I am still alive. However, I am not so well, and I think I have no more to live so long. . . . But, as God will do we will not meet again on this earth but in the heaven our spirits will enjoy when God allows. . . .

   Your sincere brother-in-law Wolf Wunderlich.

By 1870 Cottonwood Falls had almost 400 people, three dry goods stores, a drug store, three boardinghouses, two real estate offices, two wagon and carriage shops, and other establishments of commerce, including lawyers, doctors, and preachers. By 1874 there were 1,274 school children in the county and forty-nine teachers.

Johann Rogler died on March 16, 1877 in Chase County.

By 1878 life had begun to improve for the Roglers. Charles, at least, was able to build a frame house, possibly the first in the county. In 1879 an Edison phonograph was exhibited at Cottonwood Falls, with people marveling at an instrument that could laugh, cry, and sing. In 1880, a telephone was installed in Cottonwood Falls. Catherine died on May 23, 1880.

On May 1, 1881, Kansas adopted a state law supporting prohibition.

By 1890 a prosperous agricultural community was underway, led in part by Charles who identified the best use of the region—grazing cattle. This was to become the path to wealth for many settlers in the region, including several of his sons.

As tough as life was in Kansas, it may well have been worse for the Asch branch. We will never know. At the end of World War I,

Chase County courthouse 1870s

with the Austro-Hungarian Empire no longer in existence, Asch and the surrounding region were briefly part of Weimar Germany, but then were assigned to the new state of Czechoslovakia. The town's name was now spelled Aš. Its populace was mostly German, with only a handful of native Czechs there at the time. In 1938 the Sudeten German Party, aligned with Hitler's Third Reich, took over, and shortly thereafter German troops arrived, unopposed. Asch was annexed to Germany. The U.S. army occupied Asch on April 20, 1945. The Czechs took over again, and the German citizens were expelled. No trace of the family, their graves, their future remains. The Iron Curtain fell upon the city of Asch, but quite possibly my relatives were no longer there.

Despite all the hardships they endured, my grandfather and his parents loved this country. Grandpa often told me how they couldn't wait to speak English when they arrived in the United States. He felt that anyone who arrived here and did not do the same was just lazy.

Three early families stayed in Chase County no matter what difficulties they faced—the Roglers, the Brandleys, and the Crockers. They developed a special status as the "pioneers" of our area. The Crockers lived across a small stream from the Roglers. The Brandleys lived about two miles south of Matfield Green. It was interesting how differently the families developed.

The Brandleys and the Crockers bought more and more land and cattle. They had land and cattle in Texas as well as Kansas. They intermarried. They built outstanding houses for the area.

The Roglers, focusing their efforts on civic matters, built the schools, wrote and enforced the laws, and developed the science of caring for their land and improving crops worldwide. Behind the intellectual contributions of the Roglers there was one great–and unexpected–driving force: Great-Aunt Adaline.

The little girl who had been hidden from Indians in a tree stump grew up to have an abiding love of learning and a strong belief in the ability of educated people to make a positive difference in their world. To get her education she walked each day to a one-room school house that was three miles away. Grandpa Rogler could write, but with misspellings and ungrammatical usages. He never capitalized his I's. When I asked Mother why this was, she explained that he had never gone to school. Unlike her brothers, Adaline even went to the Kansas Teachers College in Emporia. Years later, under her influence, my Mother also went there.

James and Adaline in Emporia, 1870s

I have a picture of Grandpa and Great-Aunt Adaline while she was in college. James, my grandfather, had gone to Emporia to deliver wood for Adaline to use over the winter months. This involved a 35-mile journey, each way, over unsurfaced road with a horse and wagon.

Upon graduating, Adaline taught school and in later years devoted herself to caring for her brothers and their children, inspiring many of her nieces and nephews with her love of learning.

Eventually, Great-Aunt Adaline donated land for the local Matfield Green School and she focused much of her time on the educational needs of the community. Her dream, accomplished in later years with the help of Mother, was for all the local children to at least graduate from high school. Meanwhile, Adaline's brother, Charles, helped found banks in Cottonwood Falls and Matfield Green, built a large ranching operation and raised a family that was, with Adaline's help, to be among the most influential in the area.

My branch stayed in Matfield and tilled the soil, hoping always to find a better life.

Why did Great-Aunt Adaline have such a positive impact on Charles's branch of the family? It all stems from a sad story, or maybe two sad stories.

The first is about Charles himself.

I don't remember where Grandpa Rogler and I were or how the conversation came up, but one day he told me that Johann, his father, had not known when he arrived in America that the laws differed from those in the old country. In Germany the eldest son inherited the family's money and property, and in turn was expected to look after the family. Thinking it was the same here, Johann gave all his money to Charles when he arrived in Matfield Green. Charles used these funds to buy land and cattle. He registered the land in his own name, not his father's.

As Johann, now John, became familiar with American ways, he learned that land belonged to the person who held title. He asked Charles to change the title on the land deeds to his name. Charles refused. John was furious.

Charles, 1860s

Unable—or unwilling—to claim the land from Charles, John bought the land where we lived with his son, James, my grandpa. John built a log cabin (which by the time we lived there was used as a pig pen) and moved the rest of the family to that area near the South Fork River. Eventually, all of the other children established farms on the South Fork River.

John and Charles never spoke again.

John Rogler homestead, after split with Charles

Charles, backed with these funds and some insight, prospered. As I mentioned earlier, after only a few years in the Flint Hills, he had the foresight to switch from farming to raising cattle. He and a few colleagues transformed Matfield Green into a ranching town. By the 1900s the Flint Hills had become the premier cattle-raising area in Kansas, with up to 400,000 cattle shipped each spring. Charles's ranch grew from 160 acres to 1,800 at the time of his death from pneumonia on March 23, 1888. He had founded one of the great ranching families of the Flint Hills. (One of his grandsons, Wayne, amassed over 4,000 acres.) Charles was a man of action and ideas. No doubt he would have prospered without his father's assets. That is the first story.

The second story concerns how possibly Charles was punished for the way he treated his father.

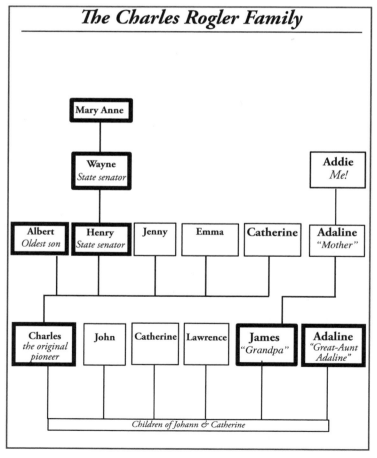

My mother told me about it from time to time. She always said that Charles was "rather rigid." He married a woman named Mary Satchell and had two boys, Albert and Henry, and three daughters, Jenny, Emma, and Catherine. Mary seems to have been ill, perhaps mentally ill, during the later years of the marriage. After Charles died at age fifty-three, Albert, his oldest son, stepped in to take care of the family.

Shortly thereafter, Mary tried to cut off the head of her youngest son, Henry, with an axe.

"I have to kill him because he is Jesus Christ," my Mother would hiss in an awe-stuck voice as she told the story; then her eyes would lock with mine to see my reaction.

I was always horrified.

Mary was sent to the Kansas State Mental Institution in Topeka, where she spent the rest of her days. Sometime afterward Mary's daughter Emma, at the age of thirteen or fourteen, also became mentally ill. She spent the rest of her life with her mother in Topeka. And this is the second story.

Meanwhile, with Mary gone, my ever-competent Great-Aunt Adaline moved in to take on the mother role. That is how she came into the lives of Charles's smart and talented children. Protected by Adaline and their older brother Albert, the family prospered.

Great-Aunt Adaline,
1870s

Great-Aunt Adaline and Albert, now responsible for the family, saw that Henry and his two other sisters all went to college. Albert never went himself, but following Great-Aunt Adaline's example he spent his life reading and thinking. He grew into a lovely man, with volumes and volumes of books. He would have made a great college professor—caring and instilling a love of learning in everyone. And in fact many of his children and grandchildren went on to become professors. This may have been a legacy of Great-Aunt Adaline.

His sister, Jennie, married a prosperous rancher, Henry Wood. At the urging of Great-Aunt Adaline, she was to play a brief but important role in my life. You will hear of this later.

The other sister, Catherine, married a college professor. Again, through this family I heard about the love of learning.

Henry, whose head had almost rolled, passed the college entrance exams, although he had never been to high school. And so the story goes, Henry became one of that "rare breed"—a college graduate who never graduated from high school. Henry graduated from Kansas State Agricultural College in 1898. He owned the farm next to Grandpa Rogler.

Henry became a Kansas state senator and had two sons. One, George, graduated from Kansas Agricultural College and did research on grass seed. He became quite well known for his work in the Dakotas and other areas of the world.

The other, Henry's older son, Wayne, was born in 1905 and also graduated from Kansas State Agricultural College. Wayne became a Kansas state senator like his father. He married the attractive blonde daughter of a rich rancher. Together they had one daughter, the exquisite Mary Ann.

Rogler Ranch 1910

Charles Rogler, 1880s

8
The Cemetery

Mother had three windows facing south. She had Dad plant zinnias, hollyhocks, and other flowers under the windows. There were always hummingbirds flying around the flowers. In back of the house there were rose bushes and lilacs and Damson plums that Grandma Rogler had brought back from the family trip to Cincinnati to visit her father.

All these plants bloomed every Decoration Day–the old name for what is now Memorial Day. On that special day we took great heavy bouquets to the family graves in the cemetery. It was a little graveyard with worn headstones bordered by tangled grass. As we walked the mile to the cemetery we chatted with our neighbors doing the same thing.

When we got there we would see the graves of the Rogler family, my great-grandparents and their four deceased children. Grandma Janette Harris Rogler, who died when I was so little, was also buried there, amid the other Rogler graves.

One Decoration Day, after we brought and laid our flower bouquets, Grandpa Rogler stood quietly looking at the grave of his oldest brother, Charles.

"Look," he said, "Charles died at age fifty-three."

Then he added softly, "And I thought he was an old man when he died."

Eventually, Grandpa Rogler was buried in that cemetery. Then Great-Aunt Adaline. And much later Mother and Dad, as well as Jim. Dad lived from September 24, 1882, until January 29, 1967. Mother always thought she would die first, but she outlived him and died in June of 1971.

Cattle Arriving at Bazaar, 1920

9
The Santa Fe and Ranching

By 1923 the United States was prosperous, and Warren G. Harding, our president, was widely popular. He died in the summer of that year, and only then did the public learn of the vast corruption of his administration. Vice President Calvin Coolidge, honest and pro-business, succeeded Harding. As the stock market continued to rise, he refused to tighten speculation.

It was during these good times that the Santa Fe Railway came through Matfield Green in July 1923. Two of my father's cousins, the sons of his Aunt Hattie, lived in tents on our front lawn and worked on the railroad.

Nothing mattered so much to the cattlemen as the coming of the railroad. A train stop meant that Texas cattle could be shipped directly to Matfield, and it was on these shipments that our pasture men depended for their livelihoods.

Building the railroad brought a lot of work and activity for others as well; men laid track beds, built stockyards, and opened offices. In August the first train came through. Frankly, I think only one small train actually came through on that day; but I can't be certain. Mother had Jim and me busy setting up our family celebration, so we had no time to participate.

What a celebration! Later the newspaper reported that 3,000 people were in Matfield that day. To put this in perspective, the population of the county in 1924 was a little over 4,400.

Mother and Dad had a picnic for 100 relatives and friends out on our lawn. This was the largest party I had ever seen. Jim and I gathered and husked a wash boiler full of sweet corn and prepared it for cooking. Of course, I had one of my mishaps. I ended up cutting my hand that day and getting Mother's usual adhesive tape. Still, it was a busy, fun day. Besides corn, we had fried chicken, tomatoes, great salads, and fresh fruit and watermelon.

Mostly, I remember Mother's sister, my aunt Elsie, dressing for a dance to be held in the village. Amid all the gaiety, she rolled her silk stockings below her shapely knees and pulled on fancy garters, covered with ribbons, below the rolls. This was "high fashion," she explained. I was entranced with the idea of discussing fashion with my aunt, who lived in a sophisticated college town. Tall and slimmer than Mother, her hair was carefully coiffed, not cut short and blunt like Mother's. Growing heavy and sloppy, Mother did not dress with care, and she and Dad frowned upon dancing as somewhat improper, if not an outright sin. Touching your partner, I knew, was a great sin. A shiver of forbidden delight ran through me as I looked at the rolled stockings on Elsie's legs and wondered if she would touch her partner.

Mother never instructed me about the way things are between men and woman, and with Dad being away so much and Mother's lack of pretensions, there was little for me to observe in our house. As far as I can remember, she only gave me one piece of sexual advice, if it can be called that. One day when I was 10 or 11 she took me aside and told me that there was something I should expect. One day soon I might see blood between my legs.

"Some girls get very excited," she told me, "They think they are bleeding to death; but it is normal." And that was that. I didn't learn the facts of life till I was in nursing training many years later.

Along about this time, however, Mother did develop an interest in correcting my speech.

"You speak just like the Joneses," she would say, indicating that my speech was common and had the local dialect. I would say "ya," not "you" and "winda," not "window." Mother focused more and more on enunciation. There must have been a fair amount of truth in what she said. In the fifth grade we had a spelling test. A girl friend sat in front of me.

We were asked to spell "forget" on the test. I did.
"F E R G I T."

My friend spelled it the same way. After the teacher graded the tests, she sadly noted that some cheating had gone on—even the misspelled words were spelled the same. I squirmed in my seat but the tactful teacher didn't mention names and it never happened again.

The Santa Fe railroad stop in Matfield marked a big change for our family. Following close upon that first puny train, the engines began to arrive with maybe 150 cars packed with steers. Sometimes these were Texas longhorns with three- and four-foot horn spans. They were taken from our local stockyard and driven out to feed on the tender spring bluegrass of the Flint Hills pastures. The grass was so high in protein that the animals quickly fattened for market.

To move the cattle from the stockyards in town out into the pastures a road was built along the border of our farm. This replaced a trail that used to lead to our place. Every year, thousands of cattle traveled this road, away from the main highways.

These beasts were noisy; they left their "soil" and had pungent smells. They were raised on "big free land" areas in Texas and may never have seen a man until they were rounded up to be shipped to Kansas. I remember seeing one nasty creature hook a truck radiator with its big long horns, even as cowboys on horseback tried to control it. Steam erupted and it seemed to me to be coming as much from the angry steer as the overheated radiator.

In the spring and fall, when we children wanted to walk to town, we carefully checked that no cattle were moving along our border to their new pastures. Sometimes we had to wait for thousands of cattle to pass. There could be maybe 2,000 head of cattle at one time—an endless river of pounding, smelly muscle and dust.

It's with these cattle that I most remember the exquisite Mary Ann Rogler. She was my second cousin, a descendant from Charles the original pioneer, and a very pretty blonde. She was a little younger than me. (See chart on page 102.)

One day at cattle-shipping time, I dallied near the stockyards by the railroad. There I saw Mary Ann riding her own horse. Close by her father, the near-famous Wayne, and some hired hands were "working" a group of cattle, deciding which ones went into what rail car. As the cars filled up, I watched Mary Ann a while, thinking what a lucky girl she was. Both her parents were rich, and she had her own saddle.

I'd been told that some of the cattle were even owned under her brand. Her father, Charles' grandson, was active in politics and was being groomed by the Republicans to run for governor.

More important to me, she was very close to her father. He seemed to adore her and took her with him when he went to tend to the cattle. I thought of those long rides with her father, and the empty spaces of time without my dad. How wonderful it would be to be like Mary Ann.

Longhorn

The Beedles, my father's family, also benefited from the coming of the Santa Fe–particularly my Uncle Roy, another "pasture man." Over six feet tall, Roy was the kind of man who commanded attention when he walked into the room. As a pasture man, he "ran cattle" for himself and others. Texas ranchers sent him their cattle to fatten on the rich, nutritious spring grass of the Flint Hills. After a summer of feasting, the animals–carrying valuable layers of heft–were shipped to market to be sold by the pound for slaughter. This meant that Uncle Roy worked very hard during the spring and summer months.

He handled cattle only from April 15 to October 16; and he handled many more cattle than Dad, about 10,000 head a season. At the standard five acres of grassland to feed a head he needed 50,000 acres of pasture for these beasts. This was about seventy-nine square miles of land to be cared for. Some he owned, and some he leased.

In late March and early April he checked barbed wire fencing along all his vast holdings to make sure animals could not get through. During this period cattlemen from Texas called anxious to know when Roy could receive a shipment of their cattle. They would agree upon a date.

About April 15 the heavy work began. At the appointed time Roy and his hired hands met the cattle at the stockyards and drove the herd to the pasture, which could be miles away.

Throughout the summer the fence had to be kept in shape, and water and salt licks provided for the cattle. After every heavy rain the fencing had to be checked and cattle counted. Sometimes lightning would strike a fence and any animal touching it would die, or lightning would strike an animal standing alone. Whenever a dead animal was found, the brand was cut off and sent with details to the insurance agency for payment.

During droughts water could be a big problem, because many pastures had ponds that would dry up. Then water had to be hauled to the cattle using water tanks on trucks.

A summer with droughts or frequent lightning storms made Uncle Roy's work much heavier. During the 1930s we had seven years of drought! Later I will tell you how hard this was on all of us.

In all of this work Roy was greatly assisted by his frail-boned wife, Grace. There were no cell phones then, so Aunt Grace, a true and

Uncle Roy and his daughter, Betty

active partner, busily covered the phones at home. The cattle owners called in their shipping orders whenever they wanted to put the cattle on the market. She coordinated much of the ranch's logistics, and the enterprise could not have thrived, as it did, without her assistance.

While she helped make shipping arrangements, Roy and his cowboys went to the pasture to cut out the cattle to be sold, drove them to the stockyards, and loaded them onto the railcars. She also made the arrangements to feed and water the cattle during this transportation process. The cattle owners didn't want a big weight loss because of the trip.

In short, Aunt Grace was part of the team, often driving out to the pasture to tell Roy of some significant news or request from their Texas clientele. Of course, during the summer, when the men needed lunch in the pasture, Aunt Grace would make it and take it to them. This is what all good farm wives did.

For six months of the year Roy and Grace worked long hard hours. Work often started by 4:30 a.m. and continued heavy throughout the day. But in the fall and winter Roy could relax and do as he wished. All the cattle left by fall.

My dad never followed this route. I think he always hoped to make his riches elsewhere through mining. So our farm stayed small and required year-round labor. Also, he must have known that Mother was too focused on her housebound intellectual life, reading and the like, to play an active supporting role. In any event, all Dad's efforts to teach Mother to drive the Model T ended in failure. She never learned to drive, so there was no way for her to do much beyond the confines of the house.

Uncle Roy was the only uncle I ever knew. He often dropped by for a chat with Dad. He would walk in off our back porch in his seasoned boots and toss his sun-bleached cowboy hat onto a counter. He was great company with a good sense of humor and great tales to tell. He and Dad were great friends. They shared a certain western humor that leveled everyone, powerful and small alike, by pointing out their common foibles and the absurdity of situations. It was a very subtle thing. I used to love to listen to them talk about some political person or other and skewer him with a witty turn. If only I could remember their words now, you would see what I mean! But it's hard to nail down these thoughts after all these years.

Roy longed for a son to help him on the ranch, but after five pregnancies, all girls, Aunt Grace said, "No more." So Roy's youngest girl learned to work alongside him. When the girls were young, he always had Shetland ponies outside the house. The ponies slept outside the girls' bedroom windows.

I adored Uncle Roy, and so did Mother.

Roy was the only pasture man she allowed to cart water from the Rogler homestead to his pastures. Also, every spring Roy and Dad would burn off the grass around our place and Roy's pastures. This was a common practice in the Flint Hills. Uncle Roy and Dad would wait for a late March or early April day with quiet breezes to burn the grass. Then they rode their horses on the side of the pasture where the wind was coming from. They lit a match and tossed it into a bunch of dried grass, and repeated this every forty feet.

Flames and smoke covered the countryside for acres, leaving the ground black and barren. After a light rain, the earth was black and moist and caked with charred remains. Another spring rain or two caused green shoots to push through, as the fertile land did its work. Then, as the grass grew strong, the cattle were put out into the pasture. The cattle were quite undernourished at this time and by eating the tender blades they gained several hundred pounds before being shipped off to market.

The same practice is still followed to this day.

I always liked and admired Aunt Grace, but her iron-willed belief in religion was a disaster for our family. Aunt Grace brought the Christian Science faith into our family. I don't know that much about the particulars of the religion, except that adherents believe the material world is an illusion and God can heal all. So, the Christian Scientists tried to cure illness by changing the "erroneous beliefs" of the sick person and embracing more fully the goodness of God. They did not go to doctors or seek medication. They prayed.

Aunt Grace was strict on the religious front, especially in dire circumstances. She lost two children when they were less than a year old. Both babies died without medical attention. Mother frequently noted this and would deftly share her observation that a doctor was present on the days Grace went into labor. Mother firmly believed in the advance of knowledge though science. Though truth to tell, she rarely took us kids to the doctor!

The Beedle Family

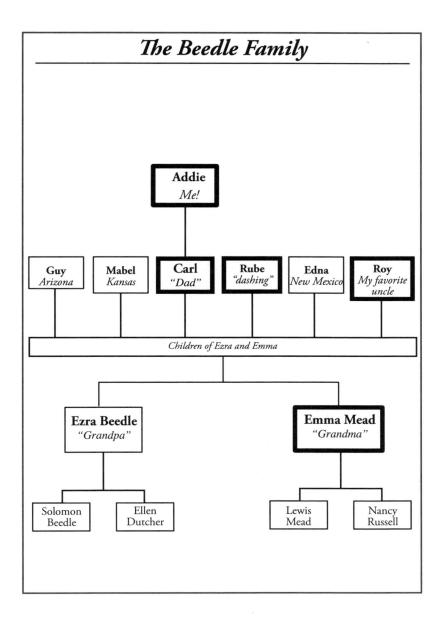

Addie
Me!

Guy
Arizona

Mabel
Kansas

Carl
"Dad"

Rube
"dashing"

Edna
New Mexico

Roy
My favorite uncle

Children of Ezra and Emma

Ezra Beedle
"Grandpa"

Emma Mead
"Grandma"

Solomon
Beedle

Ellen
Dutcher

Lewis
Mead

Nancy
Russell

Nancy Mead with Hattie and Sylvester; Lewis A. Mead during the Civil War

Grandma holding Aunt Mabel, Grandpa holding Uncle Guy

Aside from this one lapse concerning childbirth, Grace never doubted her God as far as I know. Not even when Uncle Roy was unconscious.

One day, Uncle Roy and his hired hand went out to "work over" a group of calves. Uncle Roy, like any real cowboy, was good with the lasso. When they finished, to celebrate and kick off steam, Roy threw a lasso at a young calf—just for the fun of it. The calf ran around him in a circle, entangling his horses' feet, and the horse and Uncle Roy went down.

Uncle Roy was unconscious on the ground.

Somehow the hired man hefted my six-foot-plus Uncle onto the flat back of a truck and drove him home.

"Grace, I've got Roy here and he's unconscious," he excitedly yelled as they pulled into the driveway.

"Put him to bed," she instructed. She pulled out her Bible to pray.

The hired man waited, but apparently that was all Grace planned to do. Horrified, the hired man consulted our local doctor, Dr. Titus.

"My hands are tied," Dr. Titus sadly said. "But the most important thing is to keep Roy's fluids up."

The concerned Dr. Titus devised a strategy with the hired hand. The hired man used to sneak inside the house several times a day, rouse Roy somewhat, and give him fluids. In two weeks, Roy regained consciousness.

I was never sure whether Grace was unaware of the hired hand's ministrations, or closed her eyes to them because she knew it was the right thing to do. Thank goodness Roy recovered!

Somehow Grace persuaded my father's mother, Grandma Beedle, to join the Christian Science religion. Prior to that Grandma Beedle had worked her whole life as a renowned caregiver to the sick, so I often wondered what appeal Christian Science had for her. Maybe it was as simple as that, instead of caring for people, she now could concentrate on praying for them.

I can close my eyes and see it now—Grandma Beedle, accompanied by my small, bird-boned Aunt Grace, both women with a core of steel, paying a visit on Mother. Their faces serious; their Bibles firmly clutched to their bosoms. This was usually a signal for me to scram as far away as possible. Mother sat silently as they tried to prod her toward Paradise. She would erupt in a foul mood as soon as they left. Mother always did her own thinking, and neither she, nor any of her children, converted.

If Dad happened to be home, he, too, would leave the house. His mother's neck was beginning to thicken with a goiter. Science had progressed enough so that a well-known operation could cure her. Often a son or daughter would bring up the topic of the operation, but she would stop the discussion cold. Grandma Beedle's iron-fast religious belief precluded any medical help. She prayed, and Dad was greatly distressed.

Aside from this, my exposure to religion was somewhat limited. We regarded ourselves as Christians, but without being attached to any specific denomination. None of the Roglers were particularly devout, preferring to devote their energy to community development and education. Still, Mother sent us to Sunday school every week in the Matfield community church. She dressed us in nice clothes and made sure we were clean and our hair combed. Sunday school was taught by one of our neighbors and was a rather casual affair. Mother never went to the church herself.

When we came home, a special Sunday dinner would be waiting for us—meat that was in season, fresh vegetables if in season, and best of all, in summer we had a gallon of ice cream. Mother made the cream mixture. Dad and us kids put it in a hand-turned ice cream freezer, put crushed ice around and salt, and cranked until it was all fairly solid. Then we packed the freezer with ice and more salt so that the mix would ripen and be ready for dessert after Sunday dinner. So, Sunday was more about the food than the sermon.

There was one religious event that I always waited for with anticipation. Every year or so, in the summer time, an itinerant preacher conducted a great fire-and-brimstone revival meeting in the neighborhood. This usually lasted about a week. During this period sermons were given every night. I looked forward to these meetings as something novel to do. The preacher talked about baptism, hell fire, and the need to join the church. At the end of the meetings, the new converts would march joyously though the streets for a dunk in the river.

One year I started thinking about this and the fact that none of us was baptized.

I asked Mother, "Should I be baptized?"

"Religion is a very complex situation," she replied. "I think you should wait till you are an adult to make a decision." And so I did. I never was baptized.

Later in life this caused some stress for my young daughter. She was raised Catholic, at the wishes of her father, and became concerned that I would not go to heaven due to this oversight. One year my little girl offered to baptize me herself.

I have never regretted the decision not to be baptized. In all these years, I think religion has done more harm than good.

In fact, religion is one of the few things I really have strong feelings about. Religious belief gives many people a reason to kill one another. There have been so many wars in its name. What a beautiful place our world would be if we all tried to help each other instead of focusing on whose religion is correct or best.

In our little village in Kansas, religion was a very personal thing. Because we lacked formal "year round" ministers, people often developed an offbeat type of religion, but one that worked for them. Everyone accepted the way his or her neighbor believed, and choosing something that worked for you was a very comfortable thing. Although some of the religious–particularly the Christian Scientists–were always trying to convert their neighbors to get those gold stars up in heaven; failure to convert never led to a complete rejection of the person.

You just ran into them too much, depended on them too much, and–hey–in Matfield we only had the one church to go to, so–if they went to church–you just had to pray together.

School house near Cottonwood Falls

Emma, Grandma Beedle

10
The Beedles

I always loved Grandma Beedle, my father's mother. I know I told you some about her earlier, but I'm going to tell you more. She was a dark, stylish woman with a strong face offset by the lace collars she favored. These were usually secured with a pin at her neck, which was slowly expanding in size with the growth of her untreated goiter.

She was born Emma Mead in St. Anne, Illinois. There must have been some interesting times in her family. Her father, my great-grandfather, Lewis Augustus Mead, went off to fight for the Union in the Civil War. Before he left, his wife, Nancy Russell, insisted that he sign over the farm to her. When he returned, she refused to sign the farm back into his name. Some members of the family say that a baby was born shortly after this event. Whatever went on, Lewis left for Canada and Great-Grandma Nancy stayed with the family in Illinois.

Emma worked in the Elgin watch factory and eventually met a tall slender man—Ezra Rube Beedle, my grandfather. He was born to Solomon and Ellen Beedle in Momence, Illinois, on February 14, 1854.

They married, had two children, and, following the dream of so many young couples of that time, they decided to search for good farmland. Twenty-eight-year-old Ezra and his family were the first farmer—stock raisers to settle near the headwaters of Little Cedar Creek in Chase County, Kansas. As Ezra added to his holdings they had three more children (including my father, their third child).

Then they moved to Washington State where Ezra worked in the timber industry. Another son, my beloved Uncle Roy, was born there in the city of Aberdeen. Finding lumbering too hard for Ezra,

Ezra Beedle

they returned to their land in Kansas, where they became prosperous farmers, bought houses in town, took in boarders, and lived a contented life.

As they aged and prospered, they moved to the big town of Cottonwood Falls, where several of their houses were located.

Ezra is nearly a blank to me. His father died when he was three and his mother remarried. He was raised as part of this stepfamily, so maybe he knew very little about his Beedle family.

I certainly spent time with him, but no facial features come to mind. All I recall is a man wearing slacks or a suit—never work clothes. I remember him as friendly; sometimes as reading a newspaper; but—most astonishing of all—I cannot remember him ever saying a single word, certainly not to me.

His children adored him, for reasons I will never know. And there must have been a colorful side to the family.

Many years later one of my cousins did some research into the Beedles' past. They were descended from the original Dutch settlers of New York, the original grantees of Schenectady, and early settlers of Virginia and Ohio. There must have been stories in that branch of my family to rival the stories told by the Roglers.

Through my cousin, I know of only one such story. In 1730 one of Ezra's ancestors, Direk de Duytser, owned a large tract of land in what is now Westchester County, New York. He was a Tory, and during the Revolution he wagered his farm against that of Gideon Osterhout in the belief that the British would win the war. He lost, conveyed his land to Osterhout, and emigrated to Canada in March 1785. He obtained a farm grant there, and from him sprang many Canadian Dutchers. One of these was Ellen who married my great-grandfather Solomon Beedle in Illinois.

There may be a bit more to the story, but the details are no longer known. Direk and Gideon were brothers-in-law, and the Dutcher family farm was divided between them. Direk was a known Tory who had been exiled to New Hampshire during the Revolutionary war by the Committee of Correspondence, apparently because he was a spy, or suspected of spying. The Patriots were seizing Tory lands. It looks to me, in hindsight, that Direk thought it better to give the property to his in-law than to let the state take it. Then he left for Canada, where the British, whom he had supported during the Revolution, provided him with new lands.

I wish I knew more about this branch of my family.

Years later the people of Chase County would say, "The Beedles tell you nothing." Well, the Beedle family certainly got this trait from their dad! It must have been such a contrast to the gossiping Roglers!

Grandma Beedle, by contrast, was a force of nature and an inspiration. She was a supremely competent woman. She was a doer, always helping people. Mother told me about what a great nurse she was when her neighbors were sick and how she delivered their children when their time came. When the family was lumbering in Washington, she had her last child, my uncle Roy. Mother told how she delivered herself, without a doctor, in the outhouse. She was so self-assured!

Of course, all this work as a nurse and midwife was before her conversion to the Christian Science religion.

Occasionally Grandma Beedle and her sister, Aunt Hattie, visited us for several days in Matfield Green. I thought they were great. During each visit, they cleaned the house and washed down the furniture. They were like magicians in the kitchen, taking the same ordinary ingredients we used every day and turning them into something to be

Emma, Louiva and Hattie, the Mead sisters

longed for, for the rest of your life. They made doughnuts. Whatever they did, they did well. When they left I would be sad.

Mother always was grumpy after their visits. She said they destroyed the finish on her furniture.

One time when I was five or six, Grandma Beedle took me off the farm to stay in Cottonwood for a week. I spent the days just following her around like a little shadow. She took me to visit her friends, where we sometimes quilted, and she showed me how to cook. The way she cooked was so different from my mother's way. Grandma made cream sauces for vegetables and seasoned everything expertly.

While Mother would always make angel food cakes, Grandma would bake many different kinds of cakes, including wonderful Lady Baltimore cakes. These cakes had three layers of yellow cake with different fillings between each layer—usually pineapple and chocolate if I recall. All this was covered with a seven-minute boiled white frosting. Of course, everything was beaten by hand. Grandma Beedle had me make a cake from one of her special recipes that week. Everything she made was excellent, but this was the best ever.

That week while I visited she made me a dress. She bought light blue organdy material and made ruffles for the skirt. It was the first beautiful dress I ever had.

She was proud of that dress, and maybe of me too? Anyhow, she gave me a necklace of dried rose petals and small gold beads. She also bought me white shoes and stockings. Then, making sure that every hair on my head was neat, she walked me to the studio of the local photographer. He had a big box-like camera with a drape under which his head disappeared. He told me to sit very still for a while. I tried not to squirm.

I still have the results of that photo session. It's a picture of a blond, straight-backed girl in a very starchy-fancy dress that made her feel beautiful and very special.

There was one dark note on that visit, however, in the form of a rocking chair in the bedroom where I slept. The top of its back was an oblong shape and at night it looked to me like a woman's head in the room. One night Grandma Beedle heard me crying. I was embarrassed to tell her that I was afraid of the woman in the chair. She thought I was homesick. Always considerate, the next day she arranged for me to return home to the farm. Dad came and got me.

Addie in her fancy dress

Part 3
Darkening Clouds 1924—1935

11
The Mining Days

During the summer of 1924 Dad came home and drove us to the southeastern part of Oklahoma. He was drilling at a stone quarry near Stringtown. Aunt Adaline took care of Grandpa Rogler for the summer.

Farm prices were beginning to weaken, but the overall economy was still going strong. Demand for commodities continued to run high, and the soaring stock market created the sybaritic Roaring Twenties. Although we did not participate in that type of life-style, Dad must have thought he was doing well, to take the family off the farm during the summer season.

I thought it all a great adventure. Right away when we arrived, Dad told us to wait outside the cabin while he sprayed for bedbugs. Then he took a big container of gasoline out of the car, and thoroughly sprayed the floors and wall of the cabin with a fine midst of gas. Curious, I walked along behind. And sure enough, the bugs, which were visible to the eye, disappeared as he sprayed. We did not wait for the fumes to clear; we started hauling our stuff in. The bedbugs never reappeared.

The town was segregated. The blacks (we called them "colored folk" back then) lived in the southern part, the whites in the north. Matfield Green was pure white; I had never seen a black person before, so they were somewhat of a novelty to me.

However, even in this town I almost never saw the blacks, and then only because of the Fourth of July celebration. On the Fourth, the whites had a big barbeque picnic in a park. I thought it was a great picnic. They had ball games, a tasty barbeque, and a dance with fox trot and waltz in the evening. While I enjoyed myself immensely, the blacks watched from afar. Once the whites were done eating, the black folk came and took the leftover food away. The following week, they had their picnic and dance. Of course no one from my family attended. Still, our neighbors told me they loved the music and went to listen and watch and, to my parent's horror, joined in the sinful dancing.

During August I developed a fever and jaundice, so when Labor Day came and the family went on a picnic with friends, I stayed home. I was too sick to feel sorry about missing the celebration.

The family came back that evening all light and gay. Dad joked, Mother laughed. Jim was ablaze with excitement. What was going on? In joyous tones they told me: Dad, seeing some unusual trees, had wandered from the picnic grounds. As he stood by these trees he realized that there were several kinds of ore in the ground–lead, zinc, and silver. With all his experience mining, he saw the possibilities for the place. Flush with their great good luck, Dad and his friend filed a claim to mine the area.

The light mood lasted for days.

Eventually, Mother and we children returned to Kansas by train. They continued celebrating–we were finally rich.

I didn't feel so lighthearted. I was still ill and wanted only to be back with Grandpa Rogler. I also was worried about starting school. I was the only one with a care on that journey.

Dad and his friend started to open-mine the claim. Excited letters arrived home. They were right, it was a good mine! Initial assessment of the ore showed that it was of a rich grade. Dad figured it would set us up for life. The family grew more festive and we relaxed more with each other.

Word got out around Stringtown about the big claim. Dad and his friend were toasted and congratulated. They were men of note.

Then one day Dad received a letter from a lawyer for the Humbolt Oil Company. The lawyer noted that Dad was open-mining his claim but, according to the lawyer, Dad's claim was only for shaft mining. Surprise! Humbolt had the claim for open mining.

We were away from Dad. I did not read the letters he wrote to Mother. I have no idea what he went through at this time. I only knew one thing.

Mother constantly worried that Dad would be killed.

Jim must have suffered at this time, in his own silent way. He was 13 or so and Mother had arranged for him to start high school. The principal of the school apparently did not think Jim was quite ready and decided to have him tested. Jim failed one of the tests. Mother knew nothing about this until she was confronted with the results.

Jim had not told her, had not asked for help, and had not shared with anyone that he had failed. This was to become his pattern in life: quiet suffering on his own without seeking assistance from those who might have provided it. Mother, however, was an activist. She met with the principal to express outrage that she had not been consulted. I am sure that the thought of one of her children failing in any intellectual activity was intolerable. In the end, Jim started high school, though this may not have been in his long–run best interest, as time would tell.

Not long afterwards, Dad came home, a quieter man to a quieter woman. He didn't have the money to fight big business in the courts, he said.

A few years later Mother read *Seven Iron Men: The Merritts and the Discovery of the Mesabi Range* by Paul de Kruif (New York: Harcourt, Brace, 1929), the true story of how seven brothers discovered iron ore in Minnesota, but were swindled out of their discovery by John D. Rockefeller through improper tricks by big business. When she finished the book, Mother put it down and said quietly, "This is what happened to Dad, a big company stole his riches from him."

So life went back to the way it was. We were ordinary people, leading ordinary lives.

Dad returned, not with bags of lucre, but with something that pleased me more–a frisky and friendly 'coon dog named Lady. That winter Dad, Jim and some of the local fellows often took Lady out to hunt for "fur" animals along the river. These were mostly raccoons, sometimes skunks. Also, they set traps along the river for muskrats. Any animals they caught were skinned and the skins prepared for sale. When enough skins were collected, they were shipped off to market in Kansas City.

Out in the fields or hunting, Dad seemed happy enough, but being at home was tough on him. Dad did not see eye to eye on farming with Grandpa Rogler, who owned the farm. And Mother's unspoken retaliation, after Dad's long absences from home, was usually to agree with her father. The disagreements were quiet. Dad's way was to go silent, outdoors, or off to the mines and oil fields. It left a big empty place in my heart.

So after a brief stop at home, Dad continued to seek his fortune. Most winters, when there was no farm work, he devoted himself to mining or drilling in the oil fields of Texas. How I wished there was oil in Chase County, where Matfield Green was located. But there was none. Jim and I could tell that the farm must have been an island during the time when the oil fields formed. Although we also recognized that there were times when the farm had once been under water. Walking in the fields we would find hundreds of stones with fossil imprints from that era and fossilized clamshells. They gave our water a heavy limestone undertone. But no one, ever, found oil in Chase County.

One time before he left, Dad taught Mother how to shoot a pistol, and when he was away, she always slept with it under her pillow. The nearby Santa Fe Railway caused her special concern. There was no telling what strangers those boxcars might bring our way.

She worried constantly, and, as is so often the case in our lives, she worried needlessly. Our real dangers came from nature, not man.

In April 1927, Mother woke me up in the middle of the night. A terrible storm was raging outside. A wild wind shrieked, thunder pounded. There was lightning and heavy rain. I was frightened. Together we woke Jim and Elsie Rene.

"Run outside and grab the chickens," Mother yelled over the thunder. She led the way. Grandpa stayed to comfort Elsie Rene.

Without questioning, Jim and I followed Mother's directions. Plunging into the dark, we ran to the hen house, which stood beside the edge of the steep bluff on which our house was built. Back and forth we went. We used flashlights to find and grab the sleeping chickens, and then carried them upside down by their legs into our screened-in porch. The chickens hardly stirred, even as they were tossed onto the floor. That's just the way chickens are at night. We were soaking wet, but finally all the chickens were safely on the porch.

The storm continued to howl. It was so strong; Mother became scared that our house would blow away. She led us to the entrance to the cyclone cellar—just off the back porch. Mother, Grandpa, Elsie Rene, Jim, and I huddled in the cyclone cellar. While wind howled around the house, heavy rain pelted down, and lightning flashed across the sky, we sat silent in the airless and dark space and waited grimly for what the storm would bring.

The dawn broke. Mother peeked out the door and said it was safe to come out. Fresh air and light. A deep silence, except for the hungry chickens who by this time were loudly calling for their breakfast. Debris from the flooding had washed up to the bottom of the cellar steps. Broken tree branches and waterlogged grass formed a cobweb-like mat on the few visible patches of soggy ground. The farmers along the river had lost their crops, and some would face financial ruin. Water still covered the lower parts of our land, but we were safe.

What the Indians had told Grandpa Rogler was still true. The house itself did not flood.

Silent as the air itself, we went into the house to have breakfast. We were in a little houseboat surrounded by an endless sea. There was water whichever way we looked and shifting muddy expanses laden with grass and brambles. Sometimes big branches from a tree floated past. Since we were outdoors kids, we spent the day looking out the windows, unable to work or play—or even walk out onto the porch, which was crowded with chickens. While the hours went by we commented excitedly as we watched the water recede and the wind-whipped clouds fly across the sky.

Mother was quiet. She looked at the chicken coop. Even hours after the rain, the floodwater beyond the bluff's rim continued to run swiftly past—a misstep in the dark and we would have been swept away.

Several times during the day she went to take long looks at that swiftly running water. Finally she slumped slightly.

"I'll never again risk your lives to save the chickens," she said quietly. I was so struck that she valued us—that moment has stayed with me forever.

Floods of this sort happened seven or eight times during my youth. Although the waters came up to our doorstep, the house never flooded.

After this particular flood Grandpa Rogler began to slowly deteriorate. His breath became short and labored. This was just something we accepted. Certainly we never thought about seeking medical help. You aged, you suffered, and you died.

About a year later, on June 1, 1928, the Chase County National Bank failed. Its affairs were liquidated though the spring of 1929. I heard this mentioned but had no idea what this meant. These were adult concerns that had no bearing on my world, or so it seemed to me.

Instead, at this time I thought another event was the most amazing experience in my life. Our school teacher told us that someone in town owned a radio and that all the local students would gather in the high school auditorium to hear the president give his inaugural address.

The "high school" was mostly on the second floor of the school building; the first floor being the grade school. The auditorium was on the second floor as well, with rows of wooden chairs in front of a raised platform that had black cotton curtains on both sides. This occasion was the first chance I ever had to see, or hear, a radio. On the appointed day, the students filed into the auditorium.

We were filled with anticipation. There on the stage in the middle of the open black cotton curtains was a spare wood table. On the table was a small box. We sat expectantly in our seats and after a few moments it happened: we heard a voice come out of the box, as if coming out of nowhere. It was simply unbelievable. I cannot remember a word that was said or the date, just my amazement, but in all probability it was March 4, 1925, and the speaker was Calvin Coolidge, because he was the first president whose inaugural address was broadcast on the radio.

In June 1928 Grandpa Rogler had a stroke and died in his little bed on one side of our living room. Mother found him. He was seventy-five years old.

Grandpa Rogler left his cow to me.

Mother inherited the house and fifty acres of land for her to use during her life. We children were to each share one-third after that. We were the fourth generation to own that land and, years later, the last.

I think I would have missed Grandpa something awful. But shortly after Grandpa Rogler died, our lives changed dramatically. It was as if we were shot into another world and he simply was not part of this exciting adventure.

Dad was drilling in Utah when Grandpa died. He wanted to return to his work there. Mother never wanted to leave the Rogler homestead; but with her father gone, it was hard to argue that the family should not accompany her husband. They rented the house in Matfield Green to a friend.

The animals were sold.

My cow was sold. I was not asked. I never saw the money.

We left for Utah.

Our neighbor's house in Iron Springs, with Elsie Rene on the right

12
Utah

We left for Utah in September 1928, in a Dodge touring car with running boards. If it rained you had to stop and put on curtains to keep the rain out. These were made of black leather with narrow isinglass windows. They attached with grommets that twisted to hold the curtains in place. Let me tell you that when cars had windows that rolled up and down, we thought that was a great invention!

We brought our dog, Lady, with us.

We were going 1,150 miles from Matfield Green, Kansas, to Cedar City, Utah. It's hard to believe it now, but the drive between these locations was treacherous and quite an adventure. The roads were unpaved, the terrain rough, and we ran the risk that snow would fall making the route through the mountains impassable. Dad was aware of all these considerations and thought how best to go.

He took the Monarch Pass through Colorado's Rocky Mountains, which was the quickest way to get there. The roads were graded and steep. Dad knew, that once the snows came, the pass would close for the winter. He was anxious to start. He was right. It started to snow as we were going over and the next day the road was closed for the season. But we made it through.

By that time we were in the area of Gunnison, Colorado. The roads were not surfaced. They were made of clay and it was raining. Dad would drive a few feet, then stop and dig the clay off the wheels. We children viewed this as an adventure, not the painful trip our parents were experiencing. We all slept in the car that night along with our 'coon dog, Lady. With all the other vehicles trying to make it through the pass, we had considerable company on the road that night.

The following day was drier and we made it into Utah. In a rare display of extravagance, the folks decided to stay in a motel an extra day to rest. In the morning we drove through the Wasatch Mountains. They were so beautiful. The leaves were starting to change color. I saw a pair of deer leaping across the road—the first deer I had ever seen, and they delighted me with their grace and beauty.

Finally, we arrived at Cedar City. A trip that today would take twenty hours had lasted six days.

When we checked into a motel, Mother discovered that she had left her purse at the last place. There were fireworks, because Mother always insisted that she was the careful one. I remember this because it's one of the few times I saw Mother and Dad in an outright fight. Maybe fights rarely occurred because Dad was away so much of the time.

I doubt that Mother or Dad when they were married, in 1911, understood how different they were. Mother came from a family of intellects who valued thoughts and ideas and education. They were the kind of people who described someone's education before mentioning height or hair color. Her branch of the family, unlike Charles's descendants, was not strong on action.

Whenever a new person was introduced to the family, I constantly heard, "He is a college graduate" or "He only finished eighth grade." And of course as I was growing up both Mother and Aunt Elsie would remind me, "Remember, your mother and grandmother were *both* college graduates." That was exceedingly rare in those days. I may have been the only person I knew whose family could claim this special refined status.

Dad came from a family of strong, active women and silent but friendly and progressive men. His family would say of a person, "He owns the acres by the creek" or "She won the state fair quilting contest."

There were many other differences between my parents that never boiled to the surface. Dad quietly endured this, and made a good-humored attempt to keep things smooth. Or he left. Mother, alone much of the time, turned increasingly to her books, and for companionship relied more and more on her only son.

Anyhow, that first day in Cedar City, a telephone call was made. The previous motel had the purse, and it arrived in Cedar City with all the "family cash" via parcel post. We were fortunate that the Mormons were so very, very honest.

At this time a heated presidential race was on. Herbert Hoover was running against Alfred E. Smith of New York. Smith was a Roman Catholic and in favor of lifting Prohibition. Hoover won an overwhelming victory.

Shortly after we arrived, my folks rented a house in Cedar City. How wonderful it was to have an in-door bathroom and running water in the house! We had electricity! We didn't have to use candles or lamps to read at night, as we did at home. We children started school, and Dad started drilling at Desert Mound, about thirteen miles west of Cedar City in an area rich in iron ore at the edge of the Lund desert. This was the beginning of an exciting period in our lives in which we saw a new, more polished way of life.

School was a joy to me. I loved every class, and the teachers made a fuss over me. At the end of the eighth grade, when we had our state exams, the teachers came up to me at the end of each test and asked, "Was it hard?" I knew the teachers thought that, if it was hard for me, the other students would find it hard as well. However, any pride I felt over their attention was overshadowed by something that happened during one of these tests. I was awfully good in math and science, and I did the final state math test real quick. Having nothing else to do, I walked up to my teacher, handed her my paper, and sat back down at my desk. In a few minutes she announced to the class in general, "Addie has just received 100 in her math test." I felt so proud, for a minute.

I don't want to tell you the rest, because I'm not proud of it, but my daughter says to write it. Scribbled notes began to fly onto my desk.

"How do # 5?"

"What's answer Number 2?"

They were coming fast and furious. My teacher did nothing to indicate she was aware of this, and so I responded to each scrawled note.

I'm not proud that we cheated. Maybe I don't even want this to be in my story.

I wonder if she was proud to have one of the better math classes in the state that year?

When school was out we were free to enjoy Cedar City. To my mind Cedar City was the most modern, sophisticated place in the world. It benefited from considerable resources–farming and sheep raising, as well as mining. The natural beauty of the area brought in a strong tourist trade as well. People would take the train to Cedar City, stop at the nice hotel, and then drive by car to the nearby National Parks.

We went to Zion and Bryce Canyon National Parks, and to the Grand Canyon. Every fall when we were in Utah, Dad took us camping during deer season. Then he and Jim hunted while us woman folk enjoyed the open air and the camp life. We did not work so hard and treated this whole period in our lives like a great vacation. I was thrilled that the relentless hours of farm work had ended!

The tourist trade and the locals supported a main street that was three or four blocks long, with a Ford auto agency. Dad, Jim, and I visited the showroom several times. The new Model A Ford was just coming out, and we children went repeatedly to see it. There was a movie theater also. Even more exciting, a movie had been made in the mountains east of Cedar City, called *The Shepherd of the Hills*. It was soon playing in town, causing a great commotion. This was my first movie. We all went to see it. I remember the beautiful mountain scenery more than the plot.

Indians had a store on Main Street where they sold their products. I enjoyed watching the Indian women walk from their camp outside Cedar City to the store. They came down our street two or three at a time, wearing woebegone dark cotton dresses. One day a few of them knocked at our door. They had seen that we had Lady and that she had pups. The Indian woman said they would love to have a hunting dog. The pups had been sick and only two were left. And so Dad, realizing he had no place to keep the dogs in the city, gave them Lady and her two puppies. They were thrilled!

There were other stores in town besides the Indian store, and they always had wonderful things to see and buy. At Christmas time, several of the stores featured dolls in the windows. One day, just before Christmas, Mother asked me to go to the store and buy a bottle of milk. Milk came in glass bottles in those days. Elsie Rene begged relentlessly to go in my place. But Mother kept insisting she was too little. Elsie Rene knew how to be persuasive, however. Finally worn-down, Mother gave in and handed Elsie Rene the money. She happily left to shop.

A little while later we heard her return home crying.

"Mother, I was too little!" she said as her eyes welled with tears.

She had stopped to look at a doll display, and while she stood there dreaming about the dolls, the milk bottle slipped from her hands and broke. We all had a chuckle.

I was sent to buy the milk.

In January 1929 Hoover was inaugurated. A few months later the stock market crashed and the Great Depression began. Within weeks, stocks had lost 40 percent of their value, and the trend continued for years.

As usual, I focused on and remember the simple events of my life.

One day a new stop sign was installed on the corner of the street where we lived. Dad did not notice it. On Saturday, he took the family for a ride, went through the sign, and was stopped by a policeman.

Dad explained that the sign was new and he had not noticed it. As he talked, Elsie Rene, who was six years old, began to cry louder and louder. Soon the policeman could not stand it, and let Dad off with a warning.

I turned to Elsie Rene and asked, "What were you crying about?"

"What do you mean?" she responded, "I scared him away. Didn't I?"

Then and there I realized that Elsie Rene had a trait I didn't have: she thought about managing people.

I didn't realize it at the time, but Jim and I grew apart while we were in Cedar City. There were always lots of children to play with. With these other children, we did not depend on each other so much. The local Mormon girls were beautiful and glad to include me in their activities. I joined the Sea Gulls group for young girls. Who or what Jim did during this period I could not tell you. He was home; he was studying and attending his last year of high school. He joined the Boy

Scouts and learned to play tennis. Also the boys had their own baseball team. I think he enjoyed Cedar City.

By the spring of 1929 so much land in the United States had been planted in wheat that there was a great food surplus. With Russia again exporting grain to Europe, wheat prices dropped to 75 cents a bushel. Farmers responded by planting more. They had loans and debts to repay.

Mining activity began to slow as the troubles from the rest of the world slowly made their way to Utah. Although Dad was still employed at Desert Mound, when summer came we moved into a company house at Iron Springs. This move shortened Dad's commute. He worked a 12-hour shift from 6 a.m. to 6 p.m. That summer Jim worked in the assay office of the mine. His job was to collect the ore from the railway cars and grind the samples so that the assayist could determine the quality of the ore.

Our fairy tale life in Cedar City ended, but we only thought of being with Dad. None of us said "I hate it here."

Iron Springs was about thirteen miles west of Cedar City on the edge of the Lund desert. A two-lane gravel road connected it to Cedar City. At one time there had been an iron mine, but it was already depleted. The company houses and depleted mine were about a third of a mile apart.

Coming from Cedar City, we first saw a small post office and across the road from that a small country schoolhouse. Next came a few houses and an open field used every spring for shearing sheep.

Driving a little farther, we came to the old iron mine, which had been mined using the glory hole method. The ore was removed from the bottom and went to the top of the hill on the other side. There wasn't much left except a huge hole shaped like a morning glory and a large building where the train cars had loaded the ore.

The road passed this and came to an area with six houses, three on each side of the road. In the days when Iron Springs had been a working mine, the bosses lived in these houses. When we arrived they were rented out to the workers at the Desert Mound iron mine located about three miles away.

We watched as Dad baptized one of these houses with his usual dousing of gasoline. We moved in. It was a Spartan two-bedroom cottage with one walk-in closet. Spare, beyond modesty, it did have electricity and running water—which was more than we had at home in Kansas.

The company timekeeper and his wife and newborn baby lived next-door. Many of our neighbors were Mormons. They were always gracious and pleasant. Deprived of her family, Mother began to interact increasingly with the local women. Her education set her apart. Soon, the women joined Mother in reading. More and more "cultural" reading went on in the town to the detriment of other chores. All the women thought it great to have such an educated person among them.

Dad bought an Oldsmobile car and taught Jim and me how to drive and change a tire. No driver's license was required. We fought over who would drive to school in September. Jim at sixteen was starting college. I was thirteen and in ninth grade. We would have to drive thirteen miles each way to get to our schools. Elsie Rene's school was much closer, and Dad had only a three-mile drive to work.

On Saturdays we drove to Cedar City to shop (with a long list); in the winter I did the shopping after school. In the summer food was kept cool by placing it in a wood orange crate covered with gunnysacks. On top was a can with some small holes through which water dripped. The box was placed by an open window so the air would blow past and cool the contents with evaporation. Larger establishments were cooled in much the same manner. A spray of water went into gunnysacks hung close to the windows and fans blew the air through.

The view from our new home was lovely. The Iron Springs flowed fifteen or twenty miles from our small village out into the desert; then the water sank into the sand. Every evening, as a golden awe fell upon the earth, a band of wild horses would go to drink the water. We watched them from afar. No road went into the desert, so we never could get close. They were descended from horses that had escaped from the early Spanish conquistadors. Every evening I looked at this lovely view and felt mellow and at peace.

In the winter, herds of sheep came down from the mountains to graze. They had to wait until there was snow for their water. A shepherd in a covered wagon accompanied each herd. Each herd also had a few black sheep scattered among all the others. I was told that the herder would count the black sheep rather than all the white ones, in order to know that his flock was intact. The lambs would be born here in the spring.

Then in the spring, the sheep were sheared before returning to the mountain pastures. I watched, amazed at how in only a few minutes the men could shear all that wool off. Each sheep emerged a naked, skinny thing.

On the Fourth of July, Dad drove us all to Cedar Breaks. The drive in the mountains about twenty-five miles east of Cedar City was delightful. We walked to the rim and saw a surprising, beautiful, and steep drop-off of about 2,000 feet. The canyon wall is of white, pink, and red stone. The view into the Lund desert goes on for miles. You cannot help but feel uplifted just to see what the world looks like from that height.

Dad stopped the car a few hundred feet from the rim. We all hurried to get out, except Elsie Rene who refused to budge from the car. Mother tried to coax her out. She told Elsie Rene how beautiful the view was. Mother begged. Nothing worked. Elsie Rene looked fear-stricken and cried harder and harder.

Finally Mother said, "I'll give you a dollar if you will take a look."

Elsie Rene's tears stopped. She got out of the car, walked to the rim, and enjoyed the view.

When we returned to the car I said, "See, there was nothing to cry about."

Her eyes widened at my stupidity.

"Well, I got a dollar; didn't I?" was her guileless reply.

I could not argue. No one could argue with Elsie Rene.

In 1930 the price of iron ore dropped and the company decided to close Desert Mound. This I remember. I did not hear that 4.5 million people were out of work, nor did I hear President Hoover assure the nation that the bad times would pass in six months.

At this time my family was not particularly concerned about the economy—we had seen ups and downs before.

Fortunately for us, however, the same family that owned Desert Mound also had an old gold mine in Pioche, Nevada. They thought they could run low-grade gold ore through a crusher and make a better-grade ore that would pay off.

The summer of 1930 we moved to Pioche, Nevada, so that Dad could work in this mine as an ore sorter. (He picked low quality ore off of the conveyor belt, leaving only the higher quality to be processed.) There were no houses available in Pioche itself, so Dad and a friend of his who was a driller, Mr. Ashburgh, found two houses available at another mining area that was relatively close by. This area, the Prince Mines, was about three and a half miles from Pioche via a switchback road over hills or seven miles by an easier route.

Close to the old Prince mine there was a row of five houses, and then another group of three houses and a boarding house clustered a little way off.

There were people from all over the United States in those few houses. As an educated woman and a teacher, Mother again became an important person in the community. She was perfecting a role that she loved. One constant theme, harking back to Great-Aunt Adaline, was the importance of education. Naturally, the mine camp wives under Mother's influence spent their free time reading. But Mother also carved out a role for herself as the expert and authority on many matters, particularly child rearing.

Mr. Tom Wah ran the boarding house. Mother frequently sent me over to the boarding house to buy a loaf of his fresh-made bread. As I waited among the long wooden tables, he once told me that he had sent to China for a wife and was excitedly awaiting her arrival. Eventually she appeared; a tiny little thing, with short black hair and speaking little English. In time she had a baby. Without relatives or experience, she had no idea how to care for it. It cried and cried. Nursing, as I recall, was a problem.

Within a day or so, Mr. Wah sent his wife over to our house. She came one morning with the baby in her arms. Maternal instinct, I guess, gets you only so far. (Although I could say the same thing about Mother.) Mrs. Wah was always at our house asking Mother how to handle the baby.

"The poor girl," sighed Mother, "she has no education!"

The baby thrived, enhancing Mother's reputation.

Next-door was a young couple from California, Andy and Nellie. We were neighborly. And the wife, Nellie, also came to Mother when she had any problems with their two small children.

There was another couple, Ira and Gertrude, Midwesterners like ourselves. They liked to play poker for matches, so every Saturday night Dad, Jim and I would go over to their house for a game of poker.

"Good folks, hard working," said Dad.

Not too far away in Pioche, where Dad worked in the mine, there was a saloon that also had gambling. I was never allowed in it and never went. But every now and then Gertrude would come crying to Mother that Ira had lost money there. One day she came to Mother with a different tale. She had played a slot machine and lost so much she was afraid to tell her husband. I don't remember Mother's advice.

The Ashbaughs, Dad's friends, had the house between our house and the old mine buildings. One Thanksgiving they came to our house for dinner. The next one they invited us to theirs.

Mrs. Ashbaugh wanted a big turkey for this special dinner, so she decided to drive to a turkey farm to pick out the biggest bird she could find. She visited every turkey farm within a ten-mile radius in their Model T. Finally selecting the perfect bird, she brought it home a few days before Thanksgiving.

She put it in a little building nearby and gave it food and water. Then she began to worry that it wasn't getting enough exercise. So she let it go out for a run. It refused to return to the little building.

In the evening as the bedraggled men returned from the mine, they all chased that turkey for the longest time. If she wanted the bird to have exercise, it sure got it.

Once caught, the turkey was never let outside again. And thus its last days were spent in solitary confinement, if you will. Mrs. Ashbaugh and that bird created a great dinner for us. The browned and under-exercised meat was tender and tasty!

"Can really cook," said Dad.

The Ashbaughs did not have any children, and I, attracted to any woman who could value me, used to visit Mrs. Ashbaugh a lot. Whenever I felt like it I would walk over and knock on the door. She'd call "Come in" and ask, "What have you been doing?" in her rough voice. She was tall, a little on the heavy side and very opinionated. We would sit in her kitchen and talk, nothing fancy, just the goings-on in our little mining community. Sometimes she would take me on drives when she went shopping.

150

In the early summer when the sego lilies were in bloom, I wandered the desert scrub to pick them. And so I might bring a small bouquet to Mrs. Ashbaugh, or home to put in a water glass on our kitchen table. The lilies grew at the base of the sagebrush, buried deep into the soil. In spring, a grass-like blade broke open the ground, and soon a simple lily followed, about 6 inches high. They had three jaunty white petals, with a deep red brush at the base and a yellow center. I loved these pure flowers; sturdy survivors that they were.

Labor Day was the big celebration day in our area. It was the biggest holiday of the year, and everyone loved it. On Christmas there was time off and modest decorations. And of course a really nice meal and maybe a present. But the whole area celebrated together on Labor Day. No one worked. The men all said, "This is our holiday" as they strongly identified themselves as "labor."

To encourage the celebration the mining companies threw a big party in Pioche. Everyone gravitated there to participate in all the action: a big barbeque with potato salad, sandwiches, sausage and hamburgers, followed by throwing contests with prizes and boxing contests. Everything was free.

In my mind, Pioche had action most days, in any event. There was a saloon in town and also a house at the north end of town that constituted the "red light" district. All this was common knowledge; the locals frequently discussed the merits of both institutions. Prohibition was still in force in the United States, but of course liquor was served in the saloon. Walking in Pioche I sometimes heard groups of townsmen discussing what they would do if a federal officer arrived—deny the existence of alcohol, of course. However, I never heard of an officer arriving. With the deepening Depression, no one cared much about Prohibition. As to the town's red light district, there was a general consensus on this. The men believed that the little house made the area safer for women, and so they encouraged it. Occasionally a Pioche woman would also say to me, "Miners and other men around without a woman? That house protects us."

Mother and Dad never mentioned this aspect of Pioche to me; but it was clear to me that I should focus my visits there on the business district. A careful and obedient girl, I did this.

On our first Labor Day in the area, our whole family went to Pioche for the barbeque. Then we sauntered over to the center of town where a platform was set up to watch the local men participate in boxing matches. Boxing was a big part of our recreation in those days. Dad had even bought Jim two sets of boxing gloves so that they could box together in the evenings. When the gloves first arrived, I insisted that I be given the chance to box against Jim as well. He quickly gave me a bloody nose, ending my career but not my enthusiasm for the sport. I always listened to the boxing matches on the radio if I could, right along with the men. I thought about this as we watched the matches that Labor Day, and then suddenly realized that I was alone with Mother and Elsie Rene. Where were Dad and Jim? I was puzzled, but too engaged with the boxing to think much about their absence. Suddenly, Jim came running up to me, catching his breath. He had a big grin on his face.

"Put your hands in my pockets," he instructed. But before I did, he put his hands deep into the lumpy pockets of his overalls and, half pulling his elbows up, showed me big palms full of silver dollars. He quickly let these slide back into his pockets where they would remain unseen.

"Dad is in the saloon," he said, "gambling and winning big!" Mom and Elsie Rene heard this too. We had thought the day was great, but now we were thrilled. When Dad joined us his pockets were also bulging. Dad won big that day, and we went home with food money for several weeks. What a happy fun day it was.

Today as I wrote this I thought of the whole family with smiling faces and how we enjoyed that day. It almost came back to me, as if it had just happened. Then I stopped and realized, of the five in the family that beautiful Labor Day, I am the only one living. The last one of the family to die was my sister, and that was 16 years ago.

Over time I realized that Dad's Labor Day visit to the saloon was no aberration. Dad often stepped into the saloon. My impression was that there was always a game going on. I never heard of him losing any money. He only told us he had played when his pockets were filled with silver dollars.

In September Jim returned to Cedar City for his second year of college. I started my second year of high school in Panaca, Nevada—

the closest high school. For a short few months Dad would drive me to Pioche each morning on his way to work and from there I took the school bus to Panaca. It was jammed packed with high school students from all over the county.

Dad continued to work at the gold mine in Pioche. The livelihood of so many people depended on that enricher turning poor-grade ore into high-quality ore. Late that fall, the gold ore enricher was ready to work. They processed one railroad car of ore. Before we could really relax and celebrate this good turn of events, the processing plant burned down. There were many rumors as to why it burned down. The most prevalent was arson. The Depression was causing even gold to drop in price. The bottom line: Dad was unemployed.

There was some discussion between Mother and Dad. The Prince Mine about a mile from where we lived needed men for shaft mining, but she didn't want him to work underground. Eventually, Dad was hired as a "top man" at the Prince Mine. I'm not sure what that meant, but I know he did not go down into the mine.

Since Dad was no longer working in the gold mine near Pioche, I started boarding in Panaca during the school year so I could be near my high school. It was 1930 and I was fifteen. We looked for a place for me to board during the week and settled on a rooming house recommended by the school administration. I boarded with a Mormon family, Mr. and Mrs. Edwards. They ran a boarding house just for high school students, as Panaca had the only high school in the whole county. They had a two-story white clapboard house, with electric lights but no bathroom. (I used to wash up only on the weekends when I returned home.) They had several boarders; the boys stayed in a shed out back and the girls slept in bedrooms on the second floor.

The Edwards had a daughter, Marie, whose room I shared. We became quite friendly. Frequently the two of us would visit Mrs. Edwards' two bachelor brothers who lived across the street. They had a radio; we didn't. Although, as mentioned earlier, I had once listened to a presidential speech over the radio in the Matfield Green high school, this was my first chance to really hear a radio in a home. Marie and I listened to *Amos 'n Andy* every week on the radio. The Edwards only had one other child, a son, and he was away on his "mission"—something required of every young Mormon man of a certain age. Mostly,

I focused on my school courses. I loved to learn everything I could and started taking extra courses every chance I got. It was not for the grades, which were good but not stellar, it was for the love of learning—especially math and science. I just could not learn enough.

Every day Mrs. Edwards cooked three meals for us, and lunch was always a big hot meal. With all those teenagers around, you might think that Mrs. Edwards would get frazzled now and then, but nothing upset Mrs. Edwards. She was always gracious and kind. In all the time I stayed with her, I remember only one slight aberration in her demeanor.

One day I was helping her in the kitchen, along with some of the other girls. It was rare for her to try to instruct us in any manner, but that day she was talking to us about modesty. I have no idea why the subject came up or why she decided to get personal. In the middle of the kitchen, in front of all the girls, she started discussing modesty.

"I am very modest," she pointedly proclaimed. "In fact, my husband has never seen me naked."

The kitchen went silent. I was shocked that the subject even came up. People did not talk about such things when I was growing up.

Now all I can think is: no wonder that couple only had two children.

I was in my second year of high school and beginning to be aware of how I looked. I was very blonde, with blue eyes that shone amazingly when I wore the color blue. Blue became my favorite color. My wardrobe was limited, but every dress I made for myself that year was blue. Dark blue, light blue—my eyes reflected them all with great effect! And I was experimenting with as many flattering shades as possible.

I joined the school orchestra that year and played third violin. Given that numerous childhood earaches had impaired my sense of hearing, this was not one of my finer efforts. Toward the end of the school year we took pictures for the yearbook and I was to be part of the orchestra picture. We were instructed the day before to wear a black dress to school for the picture the next day. I went back to the rooming house and looked at my clothes in the closet I shared with Marie. I remembered having ruined the Beedle family party so many years ago by cutting my hair into a triangle. What to do? I had four or five dresses, but they were all blue. I decided to wear my best dress to school, because this was going to be a formal picture. It was light blue.

I hardly slept that night, worrying that I was about to ruin another important photo opportunity.

However, when I showed up in class, no one said anything, to my relief. The picture was taken. Also, the photographer took individual pictures of each student for the yearbook. I was happy the incident passed without comment, but still had a slightly queasy feeling about what the pictures would look like. Later, when the developed orchestra print was ready, I was thrilled! I looked like a star!

I still wear blue today, and it still makes my eyes shine. Blue is my favorite color.

I found this out about the color blue all on my own. Mother would never think about what makes you look good. The Roglers did not emphasis appearance and looks all that much. Dad was silent about his immediate family, as well. So when I was a child no one ever told me I was good looking, certainly not at home—or discussed how to make yourself look better.

Only decades later as an old woman, did I learn from a cousin that in my youth I was considered a great beauty. Funny, now that I am in my 90s people always tell me that I am beautiful! It's still my blue eyes that they are focusing on.

We were given the chance to purchase the pictures and I bought my individual one for Mother, using money saved from my allowance. That Friday night when I returned home to Pioche, I gave it to her. She placed it on a little shelf in the living room wall. I woke up the next morning and was walking through the living room to the kitchen, where Mother was at the wood stove. She had my picture in her hands. We had not said a word to each other; we had not said good morning.

"I'm not going to have your eyes following me all day long," she said. She threw the picture into the wood stove. As the flames licked my face in the photo, I turned and walked out the door. I went for a walk or to visit Mrs. Ashbaugh. There is a reason why I am strong.

Panaca High School Orchestra, spring 1930

Addie on right, second row from bottom

While we lived in Pioche and I boarded with the Edwards, Jim lived in a boarding house in Cedar City so that he could finish his last year of junior college. Jim and I rarely saw one another, and when we did it was just in passing.

He was by far the youngest in his class, and although his grades were great, he had no social life. He was too young, in any event, for the few girls in the college—even when he graduated, he was just seventeen. Mother, like all the Roglers, always told us kids that education and grades were everything; I think Jim was about to learn that this was just not so. Sometimes drive and common sense are required in life.

I was home in Pioche one weekend when Mother received a letter from the woman who ran the house where Jim boarded. The disturbing news was that Jim had failed, for quite a while, to pay his room and board.

Mother was puzzled. She and Dad had given Jim more than enough money when he was last at home. There were no phones. Immediately, my parents got in the car and drove to Cedar City to see Jim.

Jim told them he had broken his arm playing basketball, needed funds for a doctor, and had used the money on hand. Wanting to assert his independence or maybe copying Dad, he tried to make up the loss by playing poker. He kept losing, until everything was gone. And then, of course, he was too embarrassed or scared to tell.

After hearing the story, Mother made everything right.

This was what my brother was to become—a man who never did learn to ask for help. He preferred to figure out how to handle things in his own way. Later, when things did not work out as he planned, he would smolder in silence.

After graduation from his two-year college Jim returned to Pioche and worked with Dad in the mines during the day. He spent most of the evenings reading with Mother. There was no one his own age in the vicinity and his main recreation was playing cards for matches with family and neighbors. Jim, the smartest of us children, was drifting without any stimulation of even the most basic sort.

My brother Jim

Rube Beedle and his wife

13
The Beedle Ranch

Around this time, Ezra Beedle, my quiet grandfather, died. He was a silent man, but his children adored him. He must have had some real qualities that I never knew.

After Ezra died, Grandma Beedle repeatedly asked us to return to Kansas. Mother, always homesick, desperately wanted to return to the Flint Hills, and this provided additional ammunition. Dad could not say no to both his wife and his mother. In the spring of 1931, Dad agreed to return to Kansas and live on his mother's ranch.

Maybe other factors had some weight in this decision as well. During the three years we spent away, a deep depression spread throughout the world. By 1931 the threatened financial collapse of Western Europe brought a new wave of deflation to the United States. Not long after we left, the Prince Mine, where Dad last worked, was closed. By September 1931, most European countries had devalued their currencies and gone off the gold standard.

In 1931, a total of 2,294 banks failed and 12 million people were out of work. A large wheat harvest in 1931, made possible with the help of the tractor and the ripping up of the western plains grasslands, produced less at market than it cost to produce. The Depression worsened. But the rolling clouds of economic distress were far from my thoughts or comprehension at that time.

I struggled with two potent but conflicting emotions: sadness at the thought of leaving Mrs. Ashbaugh, whom I had come to care for deeply, competed with my youthful excitement about our return trip to Kansas. I was especially excited about a planned visit with my uncle in Arizona and his family.

To help us on this trip Dad bought a two-wheel trailer and had a hitch put on the car so we could take some of our things "home" with us. We began to lug bags and trunks into the trailer.

As we were busy packing, Mrs. Ashbaugh called me to her kitchen. She put her ample arms around me.

"I have something to give you," she said, her voice huskier than usual.

It was a beautiful Indian basket, made of fine reeds with a zig-zag design.

"An Indian woman gave this to me in Nevada," she said, "in 1915—the year you were born. I'm giving it to you so you will remember me."

Throughout the trip I carried my Indian basket from Mrs. Ashbaugh on my lap, carefully wrapped in a blanket. That one treasure survived our trip back to Matfield. It survives to this very day.

The rest of our possessions were loaded in the trailer. This included my violin, which got wet and fell apart during the journey. It was tossed in the trash once we arrived in Kansas.

Many years later in the 1980s Elsie Rene and I returned to visit the Prince Mines and Pioche. The mines were not open and only a handful of people lived in the area. The houses by the Prince Mines were falling down onto dusty fences with "Keep Out" signs askew. I couldn't imagine ever living there. However, the sagebrush was still growing and, at the base of each brush, the sego lilies were there–just like 50 years earlier! Mankind had taken the precious ore and moved on. The sagebrush and the lilies endured.

A little breeze rushed past the sage, producing a husky tone.

"Mrs. Ashbaugh," I thought, "I remember."

Dad had a brother, Guy, who worked in the copper mines in Miami, Arizona. Dad and Guy had not seen each other for many years. So we took the "southern way" back to Kansas–through Arizona. We left in February. This gave us plenty of time to be back in Chase County by March 1. Farm families always need to be on their farms by March 1 for spring planting.

The first day of the trip was unforgettable. The road was a dirt trail littered with big stones. With relentless punctuality, the trailer's tires kept going flat. Dad repaired the tires constantly. He never got angry or frustrated. He just calmly got out and did what needed to be done. I always thought his endurance and calm were remarkable.

We went through Las Vegas, a sleepy little town with big signs saying CHECKS CASHED HERE. This was a convenience for the workers then busily constructing the Boulder Dam in the Colorado River.

Finally we made our way to Needles, California–the first point where we could cross the Colorado River on a ferry. We stopped at Phoenix for a pleasant one-day rest, and then drove through the beautiful mountainous area where Uncle Guy's family lived.

This would be my only visit with that side of the family. And they were wonderful!

You may wonder why Dad's family was so far-flung. Dad was one of six children, and they lived all over the Midwest, as the chart on page 117 shows.

Aunt Edna and David

Uncle Roy, age 27

Grandma (with goiter), Aunt Mabel (on right)
and Mabel's son and grandson

Of course, Uncle Roy, the youngest child and a pasture man, lived in Bazaar, Kansas, with his wife Grace. Uncle Guy worked in a copper mine in Arizona. Aunt Edna lived on a ranch in New Mexico. Aunt Mabel lived in New Mexico, where she raised beans until Grandpa died and she moved back to Kansas to help on his farm. Somehow, Mabel and Grandma did not get along during Mabel's stay on the Beedle ranch. I never heard the story. I think Grandma may have blamed the poor receipts from the farm on Mable and her family, not understanding that the weakening economy was bigger than any one family. Uncle Rube ran a cotton ranch in Arizona till it failed in the Depression; then he moved his wife and ten children to Idaho where he looked for work. Rube was the "dashing" one of the family. I never met him, but Dad told me that Rube, sure of his wholesome good looks, would swagger and always carry a revolver as a young man.

The size of Rube's family was a sore point with Grandma Beedle, who begged him constantly to stop having children. As the economy worsened and the size of his family grew, Grandma decided she had to have a conversation with him on this delicate subject.

He listened politely. When she was done he gave only a short response.

"I'm a passionate man."

Not satisfied with this, Grandma decided to talk to her daughter-in-law.

"I'm a passionate woman," was her only reply.

Grandma was scandalized by their reactions—no one ever mentioned passion in our circles—but could do no more. Others in the family tittered as she sputtered on about her conversations. Still, as we started our drive back to Kansas, Rube had gone three years without adding a new mouth to feed, and Grandma was relieved. Maybe her conversations had had the intended effect.

Despite the distances, the difficulty of automobile travel in those days, the inadequacy of telephone service and the lack of an electronic means of communicating, the far-flung Beedle family kept in touch through round-robin letters. One family member wrote a letter to someone else in the family. The recipient added his or her own letter to the first and mailed the package to the next family member, and so on according to a timeworn schedule. Eventually each letter passed though all the households. It was by this means that we learned of daily happenings, such as births, illnesses, and crops.

We always eagerly anticipated the round-robin at our house. As soon as it was brought from the post office, Mother opened and read it. Then, as each member of the family came home, they read it too. Whatever news it contained was discussed at length.

Communication was different then, but it was not taken lightly; it had to be worked on. And each precious communication was treasured. From these letters we learned a lot about what our adults were thinking and what they thought mattered in the world. The focus in the Beedle family, and in their letters, was mainly on the present—not the past or future; on actions, not ideas.

For our part, a few days after the round-robin arrived, Dad would sit down and write a letter telling what was happening at our home, including weather, crops, markets, health, and how we felt about things. We discussed these matters as well, and what to include and say. When weighed at the post office, these fat envelopes always needed extra postage. No doubt Dad wrote to his family about our plans to relocate on the Beedle Ranch, and of our visit with Gus and his family.

We arrived back in Kansas from our travels in Utah, Nevada, and Arizona on March 1, the traditional moving day for farm people who need to be settled in before the spring planting season starts. I was dropped off, with a suitcase, at the apartment in Cottonwood Falls where Grandma Beedle lived. I was to stay with her while I finished high school. I was eager to start. Grandma met us on the front porch. We chatted a while, then I grabbed my suitcase out of the trailer and brought it to the closet I would share with Grandma. I would sleep on the couch in her living room.

I had missed over two weeks of schooling during our trip and move. This was my third year of high school. One in Cedar City, one in Panaca, and a part of this third year from September to February in Nevada. Standing before the principal's desk on my first day at the new school, I told him that I thought I had enough credits to graduate at the end of the year. The principle agreed. Good! I thought. I will graduate and move on.

After dropping me off, the rest of the family continued the drive out to the Beedle ranch to set up the house and look after some livestock that Uncle Roy had bought for Dad. Aunt Mabel and her family had bought a grain business near the home of her mother-in-law and Mabel and her husband operated the grain elevator for the rest of their lives. Elsie Rene was enrolled in a country school to finish the year. Jim took her every morning and picked her up in the afternoon. The following year I would take her back and forth by horseback.

Grandma and Grandpa Beedle were very progressive, and the Beedle ranch had its own electrical and water systems. Very few houses in rural Kansas had these luxuries.

It had a windmill that pumped water to a high storage area. From there, water was supplied to the kitchen and an indoor bathroom.

It had its own electrical system. A gas-motored engine would charge a series of batteries that then supplied 32-watt direct current throughout the house for our lighting and a refrigerator. This battery-operated set-up was the typical rural electrical system at that time in the United States, although the cities were on AC current. We had to buy special appliances that used direct current.

Shortly after our return, our neighbor in Nevada, Nellie, wrote a letter telling us that the Pioche mine had closed. She and the children went to her parents' home in California, while her husband Andy stayed in Nevada to look for work. During the Depression jobs were hard to come by and families were frequently separated. Nellie and I wrote to each other for several years.

One day a letter came from Nellie, saying that she had not heard from Andy in months. Fear, panic and anger spilled out of those pages. She didn't know what had happened to him. Months later another letter arrived. It turned out that Andy was safe–in a Nevada jail.

He had resorted to stealing after being unable to find any work, was caught, and was sent to prison, but "just couldn't tell her." I got one last letter telling me Andy was released from prison and back with his family. I never heard from Nellie again.

Keeping in touch with people, especially those a few hundred miles away, was difficult in those times.

When we came back to the Beedle ranch, there must have been some discussion about what Jim would do. He had, after all, graduated from a two-year college program and was returning to the world of the education-loving Roglers. I got some sense of how the Roglers viewed Jim's situation one time when I visited Aunt Elise, my Mother's sister, and her family for a few days in Manhattan, Kansas–the college town where they lived and Uncle Whit was a coach. They were disturbed about Jim!

My cousin Virginia, who was Jim's age, was in college. I stood by one morning as Aunt Elsie helped dress her and combed her hair. What a difference from Mother, I thought longingly. Mother was always able to think of things I could do for her while she read books and newspapers.

We were silent and content as Aunt Elsie continued styling Virginia's hair. Suddenly the topic of Jim came up.

"Tell me," said Aunt Elsie, "has Jim ever mentioned going on with college?'

"Not that I know," I replied.

"What a shame," she sighed. "If he only studied two more years he could become a county farm agent."

The thought of a future for Jim hung silent and quiet in the air. None of us spoke further.

Finishing Virginia's hair, Elsie signaled we were free to go.

As we scampered off, Virginia said to me, "She spends all her time thinking about Jim! What's going on with your mother? Why isn't she pushing him to go further?"

Good question I thought to myself. I was silent as there was only one reason I could think of–Mother did not want Jim to go to a four-year college. Yet she was a woman who claimed to value education. I thought of her father's drinking and how it gave her a great sense of insecurity–she always clung to their ranch–and then, too, our economic times were not good. If Jim were to leave she would be totally dependent on her husband, since for the most part married women could not work. And Mother was not one to seek out work in any event. So maybe Mother thought that two men would be able to provide more support than one, and Jim was anointed.

Virginia, miffed by my silence, pulled me onto the couch in the living room and, deep in the cushions of her comfortable home, told me a secret.

"Promise you won't tell," she said. "Jim is Mother's favorite. She just doesn't understand what Aunt Adaline is doing. Here she wants him to live with us."

I thought, "How different his life might be."

The next day I returned to Grandma Beedle in Cottonwood Falls. By this time she was stoop-shouldered and rounded over her goiter, which without medical attention continued to grow. Otherwise she was still elegant; she wore her gray hair in a bun at the nape of her neck, steel-framed eyeglasses, and dark conservative clothes. She was too active to ever gain weight like many of the local women. She was always tender and thoughtful to me. I became very close to her during this period.

She continued to be my model of the supremely confident, competent woman. She never doubted that she could do anything she set her mind to. Unlike Mother and the other Roglers, she did not live in the past or dwell on it. She was always planning what she would do that day. And she did so much!

She was devoted to her church, despite the disastrous consequences; her husband died of untreated hypertension and, as a Christian Scientist, she could not see a doctor to have her goiter removed. She read her Bible a lot. I never saw her read any other book. Another difference from Mother, I would think.

Grandma loved to make quilts. She had several friends in the area, so on free afternoons we would visit them and quilt.

Ladies making a quilt (1920-1939)

Since I had few friends in the area, having spent so much time away, I often went with Grandma when she visited a neighbor to work on a quilt. The quilt would be in a big frame that was seven or eight feet long. Layers of lining and padding and the quilt itself were placed on the frame. The women would lightly use a pencil to mark designs onto the top of the quilt. The designs were then sewn through all the layers to hold them altogether. There were squares in plain areas, feathers in circles, anything that pleased the quilt's owner. A great deal of emphasis was placed on making the stitches uniform in length. There was a competition to have the most even, smallest stitching. Since Grandma was a great sewer, she was much in demand. This was a great source of pride.

The framed-out quilt took up a lot of space in the room. The women sat on straight-backed chairs beside it as they quilted. The women chatted and gossiped, asking about each other's families and then went to discuss political matters. After the work was done, a light snack of tea and cookies was offered. The women always had a good time, all the while making something beautiful.

Grandma had a plan to make a quilt for each child and grandchild. When Elsie Rene went off to college, she told me that the only beautiful thing she had was the quilt Grandma had made her.

One of my prized possessions is a beautiful quilt Grandma made. Now my daughter cherishes it.

Grandma also gave me some very special fabric to use to make a comforter. This was different from a quilt, because the layers of fabric would be held together by knots, and not quilted lines.

"Let me show you this fabric we will use," said Grandma, as she pulled out folded layers of the most exquisite, thick silks in a variety of colors.

I was shocked to see anything so beautiful and luxurious.

"This was sent to me from Canada many years ago, by my Great-Aunt Louiva," she continued as she lovingly fingered the fabric. Grandma went on to explain that Louiva was a very fancy woman, married to a stockbroker. She sent the fabric from her stylish dresses to Grandma from time to time. She even danced with Prince Albert when he was visiting Canada on a trip to visit his Commonwealth. Since her stockbroker husband was so wealthy, Louiva had once come to visit Grandma by stagecoach (this being before train service existed in our area), carrying a large crystal basket all the way on her lap. The basket was proudly displayed on Grandma's table till the day she died.

"So one of these fabrics might be from the very dress she wore that evening she danced with the Prince." I was enchanted and carefully began to sew little triangles and squares into larger blocks for the comforter.

In the new high school I met a lovely girl, Janet. She had red hair, freckles, and a heart full of joy. Mother, who was friendly with her mother, told me a story about her. Janet's mother was a wealthy but lonely old maid. Of course she had no children. Her heart was empty and after discussing her feelings with Mother, she decided to adopt a child.

She went to the orphanage in Topeka, her heart pounding and her hands sweaty.

They asked what type of child she wanted to adopt.

"Give me the ugliest one you have," she responded, "the one no one else will ever want." That way, she knew, she would indeed be bettering someone who would be lost without her.

They brought out a scrawny red-haired girl, covered in freckles: Janet.

Mother's friend accepted her unconditionally and immediately returned with her by train. During the ride Janet climbed into her lap, put her head on her breast, and called her "Mama."

They never separated, giving great joy and happiness to one another. Years later a jeweler married Janet. He knew a diamond when he saw one. Far from being an ugly duckling, his wife was beautiful!

Also at Grandma's I began to participate in some of the local social activities. That spring Dad took me to a barn dance at the Ronigers—two local brothers who had a barn dance every spring, just as the old hay was cleaned out of the barn and before the new hay was placed inside. Anyone in the county could come, and news of the dance and date traveled by word of mouth. You climbed up the ladder to the hayloft and there it was! An open space filled with fiddlers and callers and lots of people joyously dancing as the steps were called.

With all the new stories and people to meet, I loved being with Grandma. As I recalled from my earlier years, she was still a great cook.

Her vegetables with cream and butter were delicious! I loved her straw-berry rhubarb cobbler, which was made special by pouring cups of heavy cream over the half-baked contents. We didn't know about calo-ries back then, we just thought, "Yummy."

At the end of every week Dad would drive into Cottonwood Falls to take Grandma and me back to the ranch for the weekend. Frequently on his trips to town, he stopped to visit his dear friend Dr. Titus. This was the very same doctor who had conspired to save Uncle Roy's life. A large man, at 6' 2" and over 200 pounds, he maintained an office on the ground floor of one of the Cottonwood Falls buildings. Dr. Titus took care of our family from the moment we returned until the day the folks died. I was a healthy kid and practically never saw a doctor after I got rid of my earaches as a little child. However, Dr. Titus was an important person and, if his methods were primitive by our standards today, his care and concern for the community were of the highest order. Of course, he had no competitors.

Returning from school for lunch one day, I was wondering what yummy thing Grandma would have for me to eat. Instead, I found her sitting on her rocking chair. Still. She was silently crying and reading her Bible. On sight my heart ached for her. She was in poor health and struggling with her huge goiter.

"Grandma, what's the matter?"

She waved a letter in her hand. It was from Uncle Rube, who had gone three years without a new child.

Between sobs, she responded.

"Uncle Rube has just had triplets."

"Oh, Uncle Rube will be OK," I tried to comfort her. "He al-ways has done well." She could not be consoled.

"I'm so embarrassed," she cried, "I can't tell anyone."

"What about my dad?"

"Not even your dad."

Grandma usually fixed lunch, but I served us both this time. She couldn't eat anything. I had to return to school, but hated to leave her.

I dashed home as soon as I could. Grandma was totally com-posed. She did not discuss Uncle Rube's letter. I looked for it to get some more information, but I never saw it again.

Of course I told Dad the next time I saw him, which was Satur-day morning as he picked us up to take us to the ranch for the weekend.

Dad immediately told his brother Roy about Rube's triplets. Before long money and clothing were on the way to the family in Idaho. Dad also offered to take one of Rube's sons to lighten the burden on the family. Rube responded, "They are all precious to me, I can't part with a one of them." And so they stayed together.

In a few short months, my high school was out and I graduated, just like the principal had agreed. At home, however, there was little discussion of what I might do. I guess I thought that college would be the next step. Mother continually reminded me, and the whole world, that both she and her mother were college graduates. But Mother said I was too young to leave home. She wanted me to stop my education and become a teacher in one of our little country schools. I had seen enough of the local schools with their potbellied stoves to know that I did not want to follow that path. I was sixteen, a high school graduate, and had nothing to do. I took each day as it came, meanwhile wondering about my future.

In any event, after my graduation, Grandma Beedle and I joined the family on the ranch. My future looked bleak.

On top of everything else, the Depression was devastating; there was no money to spend on tuition or board. No money to buy clothing.

We stayed at the Beedle ranch from March 1931 to March 1, 1932. In 1930–31 more than 3,600 banks failed. By December of 1931, 25 percent of the U.S. workforce was out of jobs.

During this time I asked myself, "What good would college do for me?" I kept thinking about Mother and my brother Jim. They both had college degrees. Mother had got her education, returned home, and lived the life we lived. Jim, now at least a junior college graduate, was doing the same work he always did on the farm, right alongside Dad. I wanted something different. I wanted out.

There was to be no Chase County Fair that year. Prices were so low that people did not have the money to attend; thus the fair would also lose money. Somehow, however, the funds were found to have a one-day fair for the children. The Depression hit with greater force. Just like Aunt Mabel and her family, we did not make money on the ranch.

Otherwise during this summer, the family spent a lot of time in the evening playing cards—pitch and rummy. If we had guests, we might play poker for matches as well. Another typical evening activity was listening to the weather and news on our new radio. My mother and dad, committed Democrats in a family of Republicans, always loved to talk about politics. Mother, Jim, and Elsie Rene also spent time reading together. Mother bought *Little Women* and other books of that sort for me to read. But I could never get through more than a page or two. While Elsie Rene and Mother read, I would be outside pacing. I was anxious about my life and spent the time wondering what to do next. What was my life to be?

Grandma, if she was there, frequently read the Bible. Dad's jaw clenched whenever he saw her pull it out, and he often would silently leave the room. His heart was breaking as her goiter grew and her breathing became more labored.

Grandma, however, found her faith more inspiring than ever. She began to talk of visiting her daughter, Aunt Edna, in New Mexico. One day she lay down for a nap. That evening she reported with excitement that God had told her to go to see Aunt Edna. She went. Soon she had a routine. If she wanted something, she would take a nap and God would tell her to do it.

During this time the family closely followed the career of Charles Lindbergh. A few years earlier, in August 1928, while Dad was home for the summer, we had seen Lindbergh. He had just completed his flight across the Atlantic Ocean to Paris. It was quite an accomplishment, and he was so young and handsome. Shortly after the flight, Lindbergh flew into Wichita, Kansas, for a public appearance. Dad decided to drive down so we could see him. I still remember the tall, slender, handsome young man stepping out of his plane; the cheers of the crowd. They drove him off for a meeting and we turned around and went back to Matfield. In all it lasted maybe 30 minutes. At home our family followed his career for years and everyone thought him a remarkable man.

"Here is a young man who dared to dream and made it come true!" I thought to myself. I thought of him frequently during the summer of 1931, as I dreamed of another life.

The new school year started but I stayed at the ranch, helping out.

Since Elsie Rene was still in school, one of my assigned tasks was to take her and pick her up each day. The schoolhouse was the typical small white building, one room with a coal-burning potbellied stove. I think the school had eight students that year. Mother wanted me to be a teacher, so maybe she thought hanging around the local school would be good for me, or inspirational.

I have to say that these trips provided some of my fondest memories, but not for the reasons Mother might have thought.

Sis and I went on horseback, on one horse. I rode in the saddle seat and Sis held on behind the seat. We rode through the prairie pasture for about thirty minutes. We had to go through pasture fences made of barbed wire strung between old posts. Dad had fixed these so that I could stop, take the barbwire off the hook, bring the horse through the fence, replace the wire, remount, and ride on. This worked because we had cowboy horses that were well-trained to stay where they are when you drop the reins to the ground.

I took Elsie Rene in the morning and picked her up in the afternoon. We often sang as we rode. We saw birds flying and galloped along with wild abandon, pretending we were free like them. Sometimes the hawks would rest on top of a hill, far away and on their own. I loved the freedom of these rides.

Otherwise, I mostly stayed on the ranch, helped around the house, and made quilts with Grandma Beedle, who was with us often. It was a different period of life for me, like an eddy in which time stands still.

As the Depression deepened, we didn't do so well at Grandma Beedle's. The drought was so deep we could hardly raise anything; and what we did raise did not pay for the cost of sending it to market. Dad could not afford to pay the rent his mother depended on. I never really heard it discussed, or at least not in any out-loud sort of way. Never knew the details. But I knew Dad couldn't pay his mother the full amount needed for her livelihood. There wasn't any Social Security at that time. Grandma was disappointed.

Mother wanted to go back to her place in Matfield Green.

In time we left and Uncle Roy took over the ranch. With his skills at ranching, and water supplied to his cattle from Mother's farm, he was able to pay the "rent" Grandma required.

Although I had already graduated from high school after only three years, Mother–ignoring Dad's frown–insisted it would be good for me to take yet another year of high school in Matfield. In my eleven years of schooling I had lived in six places and moved seven times. I wasn't thrilled about taking a fourth year of high school, but at least it bought me time–but for what?

On March 1, 1932, we returned to the Rogler farm in Matfield Green. I dreaded the thought of returning to the homestead and taking

Elsie Rene

care of the chickens.

From then on the Rogler place was home. Jim and my parents never moved again. Dad bought 160 acres of additional land and rented another 800 acres. He farmed and developed a herd of cows. His brand was a backwards C attached to a B.

This way of life is heavy hard work. In the spring the cattle are out in the pasture, but that is the time for planting.

In the fall you need to harvest the grain and hay.

In the winter, the cattle need care—feed and an ample supply of water. You have to watch for any sign of illness. With spring birthing, a cow would go off by herself but she had to be watched. Sometimes the birthing cows needed help. If Dad could do it, he would. Sometimes he had to call a vet. A cow that died wasn't worth much, so it was a financial issue.

There was always one thing that needed to be done—and that was work!

But some things were different at the Rogler homestead. Grandpa was not there. And that was a loss. However, Dad was always home. He would never leave again.

Mom purchased baby chicks, so we no longer had to tend the incubators, and best of all, tennis courts had been built on the school grounds.

During our time away, Mother had found her calling—education of the youth. She was very active in the high school the year we returned to Matfield. She was elected to the local school board and began a campaign to secure a high school education for every child in our district. She insisted on curriculum changes—home economics for girls and woodworking for boys. Typing was added to the school curriculum for all students.

She became president of the New Century Club, I think, whose club motto was "Just be Glad," and was active in the University Women's Club. She bought special clothes for the club events, more formal and dressy than any of her other outfits, which tended to be patterned cotton shifts. Of course, she continued to read avidly—the daily paper from Topeka, the *Readers' Digest*, books from the Cottonwood public library, and most anything else that came her way. She could talk about any subject, even calculus—which she taught herself in later life by reading books about it. Dinner table talk was always about world events or politics, with a strong Democratic bias.

Through these efforts, Mother was respected throughout the community. Her faith in the simple benefits of education was constant. She often discussed this with her cousin Henry, who owned the place next to ours. He had a small country school attended by his hired men's children. Mother wanted him to close it and send all the students to Matfield Green's "superior" school. She constantly nagged him on this score and pointed out how hard she had worked to improve the Matfield system, including requiring all Matfield Green teachers to be college graduates.

Henry said "no." His country school saved him money on taxes. He was so progressive in everything else; this was a shock to Mother.

"I can't imagine it," she would say shaking her head. "He cares more about money than an education!"

Mother clearly cared more about education than money—except, possibly, where her children were concerned.

Together with Great-Aunt Adaline, she hatched a plan for every child in the county to graduate from high school. As I think about it I'm not sure if this plan originated in this period, or earlier before we left for Utah. In any case, the emphasis on education was constant and the Adalines were in the forefront of this effort to better the youth. I am not sure how the word got out, but I think Mother was the one that made the idea function. When one young boy looked like he might fail his senior year, she was approached by his mother. That boy spent many an evening at our kitchen table as Mother helped him do his homework. He graduated from high school, as did every senior in the school district that year. The Adalines had achieved their goal!

As much as I resented Mother, I couldn't help but be proud that she loved education and learning so much. She gave us children the gift of her powerful curiosity, a broad spectrum on life, and the skepticism that comes from the ability to think for one's self. She was always interested in every new idea and world development.

Back in Matfield, I spent time in the garden, with the chickens, and in the house. When the farm work was heavy, I helped with the silage and other tasks. Every day I made the family beds and every day I walked to town to pick up our round-robin letters and other items of mail.

No longer close enough to visit Grandma Beedle, I resumed my practice of stopping to visit Great-Aunt Adaline on my trips to town. She lived a short distance away, about halfway between town and us. Our simple little chats continued. She was always involved with her nieces and nephews. I already told you how she stepped in when tragedy hit the family of her brother, Charles Rogler. But you should know that as other family members ran out of funds during the tough years of the Depression, she paid for several nieces and nephews to go to college.

During this time I made another discovery as a result of my daily trips to the post office. I became aware of packages that arrived from a tobacco farm in the South. I was curious about what we were receiving, and one day stayed around the house as Mother opened up the latest package. The room filled with the fragrance of tobacco leaves.

"Why the tobacco?" I asked. None of us smoked, I knew.

Little did I know! Dad used to go out to the barn after dinner, take out a pipe and all its paraphernalia, and light up. He smoked all the while I was bragging about him—even way back in my grade school class. Where he hid the gadgets I'll never know. Now it became clear that both Dad and Jim smoked—Prince Albert in a pipe when we had the funds. Mother was ordering tobacco leaves from a farmer in the South in order to save money. Dad and Jim learned to crush the leaves and stoke their pipes, as they shared a manly smoke together. After I finally learned the truth, they were allowed to smoke in the house.

As life drifted along, my recreation was anything that cost nothing—fishing, tennis, playing cards, and reading. We certainly would never have thought about shopping for things we didn't need in order to have fun, like people do today. While living in Cedar City, Jim and I learned to play tennis. This became a major part of our lives. One year I was the champion of the girls' tennis team. Jim and I also played when we had the time. He always beat me. Often kids would stop by to chat or to watch us play or play doubles. Aside from this, my interactions with Jim were limited. I was 5' 7" and weighed 118 pounds, but he always and publicly told me I was "fat." I just didn't care to be around him too much those days.

Sometimes when I had nothing else to do, I would look at old family photos Mother kept in a chest or framed on the walls of our house. One group particularly intrigued me, as they involved a branch of the family I had never seen—the Wilsons. Mother told me these were the relatives she had visited during her trip east before she married Dad.

The Wilson Cousins from Montclair, New Jersey

The Wilson Cousins

Sometimes she would chat about how they had taken her by boat to Coney Island, or how she had tasted seafood with them—even a lobster. She clearly viewed this as the trip of a lifetime, and great fun. I was intrigued. I fantasized about what this life might be like. The father was a stockbroker, and wealthy, it seemed. The people in the photos seemed content or musing as if in a life of ease. One picture, of a young wistful girl, particularly caught my attention. I wondered what her life was like as she grew older. I wondered how different it was from mine.

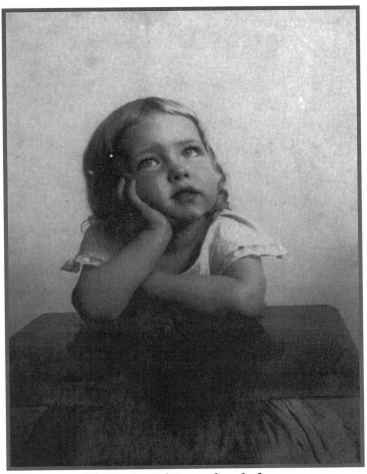

The little girl I wondered about

Elsie Rene did not figure so prominently in my life during these days. She developed a close relationship with a neighbor's daughter. They spent nearly every evening together at either one or the other's home, or walking up to the graveyard. I was itching to take action, but they were romantic dreamers.

Jim, the brightest of us children, continued working side by side with Dad on the farm. Jim would hoe in the cornfield, plow and plant, harvest and handle the cattle. If his interest strayed, Mother would always say to him, "Remember, you'll inherit everything."

Sometimes discussions came up about how to handle things on the farm—things such as what crops to plant and when to sell the cattle. Mother and Dad did not see eye-to-eye, and Mother owned the farm. Jim always supported Mother in these "discussions."

Jim was 6' 4" and scrawny, awkward, and ungainly. He never went on a date. He waited to inherit it all.

Did he ever have a chance?

One of my daily chores was to make the beds. One day I went into Jim's room to make his and found on top of the crumpled covers a letter. I was embarrassed to read it, but snuck a peek. I could see he was writing to someone saying he wanted to leave home. I quickly made the bed and left the letter on top of the tightly drawn covers.

Jim never mentioned the letter to me. It was as if it had never existed. I wondered if he ever mailed the letter? Time passed and nothing happened. And as far as I was concerned, my six-four brother lacked the guts to stand up to Mother.

At the time I found Jim's letter, I had graduated *yet again* from high school. Mother again took up her campaign—I should start looking for a job teaching in a one-room country school, teaching eight grades in one room and stoking a potbellied stove in the wintertime. I resisted.

"Mother," I pointed out, "You have always been proud that the teachers in Matfield are college graduates! I am only a high school graduate and will provide a low level of education to the whole county!"

Another option was being taken by most of the other girls in my high school class. They were getting married. From all the travelling with Dad, I had glimpsed a different world. I had no interest in the village boys and what I perceived to be a life of farm-wife drudgery, although rumor had it that a couple of them had a fight over me. Mostly, they met me through my brother, as a "friend."

Almost all of them were long-time Matfield Green residents. Everyone in Matfield Green knew everyone else very intimately, as they had grown up together. Compared to them, given all our moves as a family, I was well–traveled. I never felt as if I fully fit in.

I did have a small group of friends, even as I lacked a romantic interest.

The two I was closest to were the Vincents, the children of the schoolteacher. Our families must have had a lot in common, given the emphasis on education in both. The two Vincent children, Marjorie and Tom, would pick me up in an old car and, usually together with Edith Carres and Garrett Jackson, we would drive to visit Edith's boyfriend who lived in another part of the county. Then we would just drive around. In a way I guess I was paired up with Garrett, but I don't remember the two of us even holding hands or kissing. The Vincents did most of the pairing.

People lived and things happened to them just like everywhere else. In 1935 the Vincent children died of tuberculosis. I had never even seen them sick, but they died of it a short while after their father. Mrs. Vincent was left alone. Edith married her boyfriend in her early twenties. One day she climbed on a table to do some cleaning. She fell and broke her neck. Garrett Jackson died in an auto accident while in basic training in Florida during World War II.

Six friends. Only two of us made it out of our twenties. Now I am the only one alive, and have lived so much longer than they.

Approaching dust storm 1935

14
The Depression and the Dust Bowl 🌾

In memory I mix the dust storms and the Depression all together. In fact, to me the dust was the worst part. The Depression began in the 1930s and the first "dusters"–great storms of dust, not rain, began in 1932. Speculators who had bid up the price of land in western Kansas, eastern Colorado, and parts of Oklahoma, watched prices plummet and the rains disappear. They let the large tracts of grassland they had plowed up just go fallow. The land started to blow away.

Elsewhere around the country factories shut down en masse or operated part-time. A quarter of all workers were unemployed. A quarter of all farmers lost their farms. Voters rushed to elect Franklin Roosevelt, who promised a New Deal. By November 1933 the local newspaper reported that the list of unemployed in Chase County was growing every week.

I remember the first duster in our area–I think it was 1934. It was evening and the sky turned unusually dark, as if rain might be coming or a heavy fog was moving in. But instead of rain or moisture, great clouds of fine dry dust blew in. It was light volcanic dust from hundreds of miles away, very different from our heavier soil.

"How strange," we thought and went to bed.

A light rain followed that night. We awoke to a mud-caked world—like a drippy sandcastle at the beach. The leaves of the trees were covered in mud; so were our windows. Over eggs and ham at breakfast, we talked about the unusual thing that had happened that night. We talked about it as we went to town and when neighbors came to call that afternoon. No one could remember anything like it ever happening before. And we thought it was done. Maybe it was something we would tell people about in the future, this freaky event that occurred one night.

On July 18, 1934 the temperature was 114 degrees in the shade; a month later it was 122. Day after sunny day the temperature was over 110 degrees.

The men changed their work routine. They started on their tasks at sunrise. Then around noon, as the temperature soared, they came home for lunch and a nap. If a baseball game was on, they listened to it on the battery radio. In the early evening, the men went back outside to work. The children went swimming, except on those days when it was too hot to even think of taking the short walk to our round hole.

Only half an inch of rain fell in 1934. The dusters kept coming.

In May 1934 a great dust storm dropped mud and dirt from the western plains all over New York and Washington, D.C., and on out to sea. People farther west repeatedly found their sod houses buried in the dust. Many, including the family that was to become Elsie Rene's in-laws, moved back to our area, unable to make a go of it further to the west. These people who returned sometimes bitterly joked, "Oh look at that dust! That's just my farm blowing by."

The dusters lasted for years. They turned the day into evening.

Our dust storms were not as bad as the ones in southeastern Colorado or western Kansas, but they were bad enough.

In Chase County, the earth was faded and the sky hung heavy with dust. Our windows were kept closed, anything to help stop the intrusive dust. The air clogged your eyes and nose. After the occasional scattering of rain, the house looked as if mud balls had been splattered against its windows. And all the time, without stop, the wind labored at our windows, sprinkling the floor, the tabletops, our beds with dust. Elsewhere the federal government destroyed cattle and hogs; their price at market was less than the cost to feed them. On Sundays we were told to pray for rain, and each day in my heart I begged God for rain. Still, we were lucky. The Flint Hills had grass that firmly locked the soil in place; even during the worst of the drought our soil held. The crops were planted as usual, but without rain the harvest was small. Prices were so low that they did not cover the gas to bring our paltry crops to market.

Between 1930 and 1935 there were 750,000 bankruptcies or foreclosures in farming. In 1932 one-third of all farmers in the plains faced foreclosure for back taxes or debt; ranchers were similarly depressed. All the speculators fled. In the fall of 1932, many farmers did not plant next year's wheat; they focused on hunting and their own gardens. Half the people in the United States depended on farm production for their livelihood, and the prices were less than the cost to produce. It was devastating. The farmers that thought they could feed the world were now having a hard time feeding themselves. In the midst of this calamity the little village of Matfield Green was amazingly self-sufficient. We had fortunate geography in that there was still fertile soil, grasses to hold it down, and in some locations–including our farm–a steady stream of life-giving water.

From the bounty of our earth my family had rows and rows of canned tomatoes in the storm cellar, but there were breadlines in the cities. Mother was always afraid that a bum from the railroad–only a few years earlier a proud symbol of progress and growth–would steal in one day to get our food. When Dad was not home she kept a loaded gun on the kitchen table.

People who thought they were well-to-do, but had borrowed money against the collateral of their land, found that the land was now worth less than their loans from the banks. Many a place was sold at auction for less than the mortgage. Over the years the other early pioneer families, the Brandleys and the Crockers, had accumulated great tracts of land and cattle in Kansas and Texas. They intermarried and built houses that were outstanding for the area. Much of this wealth came from borrowed money. Then came the twenties and thirties, the time of droughts and dust storms, plus the Depression. They found themselves bankrupt.

I remember going to the auction of the Crockers' registered herd of white-faced Hereford cattle in early spring of 1931 (the first year we returned from Utah). Everyone from the area was there–even if they didn't have the money to bid themselves. The Crockers were a well-known family, an important family, and there was more than a little curiosity about what would happen. Did I say everyone? Well,

189

it was mostly men, in their overalls and cowboy boots, or in tan pants. Dad took me with him and there were only a few women present. A corral and auction platform had been set up in a clear area between the Crocker barn and the house. We gathered on several tiers of benches to watch the sale.

These were wealthy people, with a great herd, and the crowd certainly expected significant sums to pass hands. We knew that cattle of this quality were fetching up to $400 a head just a short while ago.

The auctioneer mounted his platform and started his chant, searching for bids. He went lower and lower. Silence.

He went below $100.

Dad looked surprised. The bids started low and stopped awfully quick.

Several hundred cattle were sold that day and if I recall correctly they went for less than $40 a head.

Our local Cottonwood Falls doctor, Dr. Titus, bought almost all of them.

At one point the auctioneer joked about this, "Another bought by Dr. Titus. He can pay for it next time he treats appendicitis."

But there was little laughter that day.

This was the start of Dr. Titus' own exceptional and large registered herd.

"Giveaway prices," Dad said.

Anything that went to auction was sold at giveaway prices in 1931. Congress established programs to pump money into the economy.

Our family did not escape unscathed. Albert Rogler, who had worked so hard with Great-Aunt Adaline to raise his brothers and sisters, lost his farm in 1929. He had borrowed to speculate in oil, and as we were to learn so clearly, there was no oil in Chase County. Somehow he was able to keep his home in Cottonwood Falls. From then on he became a vegetable farmer. But at this time vegetables were scarce to come by. I saw him from time to time, and he always had a nice word and greeting for me.

Dad watched all the loss and sorrow. Repeatedly he told us kids not to borrow.

"It's debt that kills you," he would note after each sale. And as the hammer came down again and again in foreclosure auctions of various sorts, he was repeatedly proved right.

"If you had your land and no debt," he'd warn, "you can find a way to survive. You can live off your land."

"Never borrow. Never, whatever the reason," he would add, nodding his head for emphasis.

"We have no debt on our land."

"Debt kills."

Property for sale, 1930s

We felt fortunate not to have any debt on our land, and to have such a fine location that, even with the drought, we could raise much of our daily needs. I gathered every bit of foodstuff that I could find. I scrounged and scrounged. Whatever I did throughout the day, I always looked for something that was edible to bring into the house. If we didn't need it for that day, Mother would can it.

When the spring came I was so hungry for something fresh that I went into the garden and pulled up the young onion shoots. They tasted delicious. If there were no young onions, I would scour the baked land and look for weeds. Some of these were edible, and we relished those plates of greens. First thing I did every morning was to go into the garden to see what I could get for us to eat that day. Every cabbage, every plant, I watched as it grew; and hoed and watered and prayed that it would make it onto our table. Each meal was a victory in its own bleak way. In the summer we collected wild gooseberries for pies, which Dad and Jim loved. The men also hunted rabbits and squirrels, so we never really went hungry.

No one could afford clothes. You bought material and you sewed an outfit and you wore it, you wore it, you wore it. I went without socks or stockings.

Off our farm everything seemed tired, slow, and sad. But on the farm we were protected.

We had seven years of drought. Although water was scarce, the South Fork River on Mother's place never went dry, just as the Indians had told my great-grandfather when he was selecting the location for his homestead. And in addition we had a cistern. So when it did rain we were able to catch the rainwater. First, we waited till the water from the roof ran clear, indicating that all the dust had run off, and then we would open the cistern.

The cistern leaked. There is a story behind this. Grandpa Rogler built it with some friends in the early years of his marriage. They made it of cement. Somehow they got to drinking too much and corn seed was mixed in with the cement. The corn sprouted after the first rain, causing cracks that never could be repaired. The precious water would flow out of these cracks during the dust bowl. Well, Grandpa never told me he ran with the Indians, but he must have. And he never told me he was an alcoholic, but he certainly was.

We always washed our hair with the rainwater from the cistern if we had it. The ground water was hard with limestone and left a thick film on our hair. To make washing with the limestone-laden water more tolerable, we rinsed our hair with vinegar.

Throughout these drought years, pasture men were always looking to use the water from our place to water their cattle. Every so often they would ride up to our house on horseback, or occasionally they came by in one of their trucks. They knocked at the back door and Mother always met them in the doorway. She never invited them inside. There would be a low-key discussion, followed by a flat "no" and goodbyes. At the next meal, Mother always reported that "so and so" had stopped by to ask for access to our water and she had turned him down. We heard and accepted this without comment. The water was very precious to her and, besides our immediate family, Mother only allowed Uncle Roy to truck water from her place to his cattle in the pastures. He tended 10,000 head of cattle in his summer pastures, even during these difficult times. The water was essential to his livelihood and that helped supply some of the "rent" he paid to Grandma Beedle as well.

Also during these drought years of the 1930s, the folks who ran the Matfield Green City Service Booster Station, which was about three miles south of our place, looked for a better water supply. The Booster Company was a private company that used water to boost the production from oil pipelines that ran through our area. They came to see Mother.

Mother didn't know what effect allowing the Booster Station to take a lot of water would have on our place. They must have expected her reply even before it came; she was known to be very protective of our water.

"No." Depleting the water would threaten our very lives.

The folks from the Booster Station went on down the river to speak to Charles' son, Henry. He gave them permission to use his water. Then they wanted permission to lay a pipe through Mother's place. She said she'd permit it only if we could irrigate our garden from the pipe. She was a tough and protective negotiator! This additional water supply from Henry's place made it possible for us to have a garden. It provided us with strawberries and vegetables during the drought.

However, even with all that extra water, things did not grow well in the blistering heat. Instead of ripening, many tomatoes turned yellow. Sunburned, they rotted quickly. We did not complain, since we were better off than so many! *

* Years later in the 1940s Matfield wanted a water system for the municipality. Henry gave the town permission to take water from his place, but drill as much as they could, they couldn't find a good water source. They came again to Mother. Dad thought he knew of a location with a good underground flow, and he was right—there was an excellent water supply. Then came the question of price. Mother thought her water was priceless, but the town threatened eminent domain. Legal rights to life-giving water had matured in the West and the town could tap our supply. Finally it was agreed that we would receive the water for our house and a small amount of cash to compensate for land that could no longer be used to grow crops.

During this time in the 1930s the newspapers and radios reported that crowds in the cities were angry and rioting. World War 1 veterans picketed the White House, and President Hoover did nothing. We who had so little felt our hearts ache for these vets.

Things were happening to us that we had no control over and they were terrible things. It was sad to think about our country, sad to hear the news.

In the midst of all this bleakness, there were moments to enjoy. On our farm we had some cushion. Every day, as in the past, I would go into the village, buy what groceries we needed, and pick up the mail for Great-Aunt Adaline and us. Then I would stop by Great-Aunt Adaline's house for a visit. Great-Aunt Adaline still owned several houses and the farm where I had been born. She continued to be active in our local bank.

Great-Aunt Adaline with her dog

Her long hair was swept into a stringy pioneer knot at the top of her head. She invariably wore a long shapeless dress, although she must have had some stylish clothes–because every year, to escape our severe winters, she would take a trip to southern Texas or to Hot Springs, Arkansas. There she took the "hot baths" for her arthritis. Spring and summer she often would be working in her garden when I arrived. She had the most beautiful flowers, even through the dust bowl. One day, as we sat in her garden, I was stuck by the colors. In the midst of this dusty gray world, she had red and yellow and green.

"Oh," I said with longing, "I would love to have a dress that has all the colors of this garden." She smiled appreciatively at my compliment.

We'd talk about many things. Of course, we'd chat about the Rogler family's history and I would hear yet again all the stories of the pioneer days. But we also talked about the goings-on about the town, and how the family was doing, and politics. Great-Aunt Adaline, like all the Roglers, except Mother, was a strident Republican.

Sometimes she mentioned in passing a thought or two about her bank–the little local bank that she owned in Matfield Green. Located on Main Street close to Snedegar's store, it had a brick front to distinguish it. Great Aunt Adaline did not like the brick front, and when she was not impressed with someone that she thought was putting on airs, she would say from time to time, "Eh, that's just like the man! He has nothing but a brick front."

I only recall one political conversation with Aunt Adaline, after all these years, and that more because she was hopping mad. I had never seen Great-Aunt Adaline this angry before; she was way quieter about expressing her emotions.

On March 5, 1933, I walked in with the mail and she was flush with anger.

"Oh, that stupid Roosevelt," she stammered, her hands in a tight fist. She had just learned that President Roosevelt had declared a bank holiday, closing all the banks throughout the United States. Any sound banks were allowed to reopen with $10,000 of insurance per account. This was the beginning of the FDIC.

Great-Aunt Adaline was furious. Her little state bank in Matfield Green had been carefully managed and was solvent.

When Roosevelt became president there was a great divide between Democrats, like my parents, and Republicans, like Great-Aunt Adaline. He really became president of this despairing country. He didn't know the answer to curing the country. But in the eyes of Democrats like my parents he began experimenting with programs to help people, and this was a comforting thought—that someone in Washington was trying to help us. I don't remember the purpose, but one program was the NRA—the National Recovery Administration. The Democrats said, "Well, let's try it. The Republicans said NRA stood for "Nuts Run America."

The Roglers constantly talked about how much they disliked FDR, except when my folks were around. They simply wanted to preserve family unity and in Matfield Green all the Rogler cousins helped one another. In this way they were remarkable. If Henry was planting or harvesting at a certain time, word would get around and the others frequently followed his lead. So there were a lot of things that the cousins agreed on. One area of general agreement, I noticed, as the government under Roosevelt began to hand out farm subsidies for crops; the whole family took as much as they could get. Whatever FDR did to help the farmers, the flinty Roglers were right there in line to get their share. I guess dislike only goes so far.

My mother and father thought President Roosevelt and his wife, Eleanor, were great and deserved much more respect than they got. And so did I. Eleanor Roosevelt was another strong woman in my life, although one that I admired from afar. She was frequently at her husband's side when he did things like having the government buy wheat and cattle to reduce the oversupply. This was most unusual for a woman at the time. The Republican papers used to say, "Why is a woman doing that?" or "The President sends his wife?" They did everything they could to drag him and her down.

I loved her and admired her tremendously. She wrote a daily newspaper column called "My Day" that I used to follow avidly. This was what a woman could do!

Later that winter, Great-Aunt Adaline took one of her annual trips to Arkansas' Hot Springs to "take the baths" for her arthritis. I visited her the first day after her return. We had our usual warm conversation and before I left she quietly handed me a package. Inside there was a red silk fabric and a colorful plaid.

196

"Now you can have an outfit with all the colors of my garden on it," she said softly.

I was thrilled.

Looking back now, the fabric itself was not that important. I think that the most important thing Great-Aunt Adaline gave me was a role model of a strong, educated woman who cared about me and showed it in the little moments of our life.

At this time, however, again graduated from high school, I didn't know what to do. But I did not think about the long term, I just thought day to day. I desperately wanted to escape the world of the dust bowl and the drought. Every time I walked down the road, the dust caused a cough in my throat. You can't imagine how horrid it was.

Finally, perhaps thinking of Great-Aunt Adaline, I told Mother that I wanted to go to college and study business. I'm not sure I even knew what a business woman might be. Even as I said it, this dream seemed impossible, and it was. My mother would not let me go.

I was on a journey; one where the direction was uncertain and no road signs were in sight.

At the time things seemed to happen of their own course, but maybe not. Maybe Mother's cousins took an interest in me. Looking back I think they were concerned about me. And because of them, I did get away, but not in the manner I visualized.

Great-Aunt Adaline and Charles's children—Henry and Jenny—became a larger part of my social life. I was asked over to Henry's more often. One day while I was visiting his house, his wife Maude and I chatted in the kitchen. She glanced in passing at a jar and lifted it to the light. "It's full of calcium," she sighed, "and I can't get the deposits cleaned out."

"Why that's easy," I told her, "just fill it with vinegar and the calcium will dissolve."

The next time I visited, she and Henry greeted me with "You should be in research! You know all about chemicals!" It made me feel proud.

I also spent time with Henry's sister, Jenny, who was married to a very prosperous rancher. Having been away so much at the mine camps, I was not close to her family and did not know her children, who were older than I was. One week, however, when Jenny was sick, she asked me to help her care for her mother-in-law, who lived with her.

I spent a week at her house taking care of the mother. The home did indeed reflect their prosperity. It was a two-story brick, with cement steps up to an open veranda on the front. There was a large and well-kept yard. Inside was equally attractive. The first floor had large, open rooms, all attractively furnished. The second floor was bedrooms and baths, and a reading room.

Throughout the week Jenny and her husband would teasingly tell me that they had heard about me on the radio and the like.

"Just heard on the radio: Adaline Beedle went uptown to buy a needle!" they would chuckle. It was good lighthearted fun, so different from home, and I enjoyed it.

One day, several months later, Great-Aunt Adaline called Mother. Henry was going to visit his sister Jenny. She suggested that I go along with him.

Henry picked me up that afternoon in his car and off we went. Henry chatted about Jenny and her daughter, who was just home from nurses' training on vacation, and other things.

I was delighted to be invited to see Marion, the daughter, who I had heard about while I visited their house earlier. As we arrived, Marion and one of her friends were talking about how much they enjoyed nursing. They laughed that they carried a bedpan in one hand and a sandwich in the other. I had never been inside a hospital, except once for a few minutes in Cedar City to visit a friend.

Naïve me! I jumped at an idea that seemed to come into my head of its own accord.

I came home and told Mother that I would become a nurse.

Nursing was an acceptable profession for women back then, and a cousin's daughter was doing it. Mother could not object. And maybe by this time she was pleased to find something I could do, since it was clear to her that I was not going to teach. Although she still thought I was too young to go to college, she knew that as a nursing student I would be closely supervised. I would live in a home for nurses under the supervision of a housemother.

I wanted to go to the best school possible. I knew nothing about nursing or getting a nursing education. Mostly in those days nurses were trained in local hospital and only a few of these were even affiliated with a university. But somehow, in a way I don't remember, I got the name of three nursing schools—one in Kansas City, Kansas, one in Topeka and one in Wichita. I mailed my applications and was accepted at all three. Bell Memorial Hospital in Kansas City was said to be the best. The University of Kansas Medical School was affiliated with it. That was the one I accepted.

I went to Dr. Titus' office for my required physical. I was a healthy young woman and this is the first time I remember going to his office. At the end on the papers he put aside his medical analysis and simply wrote that they were getting a great student. He was so gracious!

Then an obstacle appeared; Bell Memorial charged tuition. As I remember, tuition for the nursing course cost about $150 for the three-years.

That was a lot of money back then; possibly more than my parents had made in several years. I thought only of leaving, not of the burden to my folks.

Dad, his face by now carved deep with weathered lines, quietly drove to the bank in Cottonwood Falls. The man who said, "debt kills," went to the bank and borrowed money for my tuition. I was to be off!

Mother and Dad insisted that Dad take me to Kansas City and accompany me to the school.

So on a sunny day in February 1935 Dad and I took the Santa Fe "Super Chief" train to Kansas City, Missouri.

I had wanted to go alone, but Mother and Dad insisted that Dad accompany me to the school.

I wore the outfit made from Great-Aunt Adaline's flower fabric, a red jacket and skirt with a plaid blouse.

I was going to a new world.

One hundred and fifty miles in a three-hour ride, on the steam-powered Super Chief.

Destination, unknown at the time.

Next stop, my adult life.

Addie age 16

Epilogue

Grandma Beedle died during my second year of nurses training. I was home for a vacation and went to visit her. The goiter had grown, untreated in accordance with her Christian Scientist beliefs. When we saw her this time, she was worn out and sober because she was having trouble breathing. The discomfort was evident on her face. I must have talked about the hospital and all my experiences there.

Before I left she told me that she wanted me to take her to the hospital for surgery to remove the goiter. I was thrilled; this woman whom I dearly loved would let me save her life. Then, shortly before we left, she asked me to call one of her Christian Science friends.

I worried that they would try to stop the surgery.

A short while later, she asked if I had called them.

"Yes."

"What did they say?"

"They said they would pray for you," I lied.

Shortly after, Dad and I took her by train to Kansas City.

The day before the surgery the doctor visited her in her hospital room. I was by her side. As we left he pulled me aside.

"She is completely worn out," he said. "Her body is just exhausted."

I'm not sure that I took it all in, I mean what he meant by that.

The next day she had her surgery. I was scheduled to take care of her. I waited proudly to give her the best nursing care possible; love for her filled my heart. As I waited after the surgery, she was wheeled to her hospital room with a tube sticking out of her mouth. It was wrenching.

My only relief was to look away. Her trachea had collapsed. She was unable to talk, but she could see I was there. I bathed her and changed her linen. I watched them feed her intravenously. I don't remember what I felt. I felt nothing. She was increasingly sedated. Dad went back and forth between her room and the waiting room.

The doctor said that if they couldn't stabilize her trachea, she would die.

I asked the doctor, "Can you do a tracheotomy?"

The doctor's look softened as he said, "No, she would die from the infection." We had nothing to combat infections at the time—we didn't even know the concept of antibiotics.

A day or so later some people from hospital administration asked to speak to Dad alone, without me. They did not want me to hear what they discussed.

During the meeting the hospital told Dad to send me home to Matfield Green.

To care for Grandma in my stead, her daughter, Aunt Mabel came to Kansas City.

Although Mabel and Grandma did not get along, both were wonderful to me. When Aunt Mabel arrived in Kansas City, she took me for my first permanent and hair styling. My hair was long. The stylist curled it and left a braid around my head. I felt elegant and sophisticated. But it did not stop the twisted feeling in the pit of my stomach.

I took the train to Matfield alone, except for my strangely aching heart. I think I knew Grandma was going to die. Worse, there was the nagging guilt of having lied to her.

Jim met me at the train station. Our silent drive to Matfield seemed very long.

The next day the phone rang. Dad said Grandma had died and he would be home with her shortly.

She was eighty-three.

Years earlier I had lost a grandmother. This time I lost my dear friend.

A day or so after the funeral, Dad went to the bank with his remaining family to settle the estate. Grandma had disinherited Aunt Mabel. The family was shocked.

"We all share equally," said Dad. They tore up the will.

All the brothers and sisters shared equally.

That was the family she had raised. They never understood why she had done what she did, but they knew how they felt among themselves.

They knew what was right.

They saw her strengths and her foibles, as they indeed were people who had both. They let the love and the just prevail.

Albert Rogler continued to farm his vegetables. Although he saw to it that all his brothers and sisters had college degrees, the responsibility of working with Great-Aunt Adaline to support his family stopped him from receiving any formal higher education. Instead, he amassed a considerable library and became a man who loved learning and reading. He ordered encyclopedia after encyclopedia delivered to his home in Cottonwood Falls. As his sons became college professors he would visit them and beg to audit classes when he visited. Each class was a joy to him, even when he was a man in his eighties.

Henry Rogler stayed on the land. He became a "legend of ranch management" after he won the first Master Farmer award in 1927. His home, the original Rogler home site, is now a museum called Pioneer Bluffs.

Dad died in 1967. Four years later Mother died.

Jim never left home. While Mother and Dad were alive, he stayed on the Beedle farm in Matfield Green. The farm consisted of the old Rogler homestead, which Grandpa had ultimately left to us three children, 800 rented acres of pastureland, and a small 160-acre farm that Dad bought. When Mother died, Jim did come into his inheritance. By that time a potbelly had sprouted firmly on his rail-thin frame. As far as I knew during Mother's lifetime he never had a date, but he did inherit the 160-acre plot Dad had purchased.

Elsie Rene became a teacher, married, and raised two sons. In later years we traveled together. She was my dear friend until her death at the age of seventy-two. She was always a joy.

Roy and Grace Beedle's lives contained considerable tragedy. She clung to her faith with grave consequences. Their story is for someone else to write, not me.

Great-Aunt Adaline died in my second year of nursing school. She willed me her leather-bound Bible and a gold Elgin pocket watch that her husband had given her, engraved to and from. I missed her terribly.

Her legacy lived on. Many of her nieces and nephews went on to become educators, researchers, and people of learning. A love of books and a belief in higher education had been sown in those fertile Flint Hills and took root as deeply as the blue stem grass. It spread to all parts of the United States as Rogler descendants studied horticulture, history, law, and medicine.

I spent much time traveling in the years that followed. In time I would travel to six continents and 50 states, but no trip was more important than the first 150-mile journey with my father. I had two children, a boy and a girl. Both of them attended college–and beyond. There was a lot of living! But parts of me never left the Flint Hills of Kansas. I knew what it was to work hard, to be frugal. I expected too little of others, perhaps. But I also knew about the desire for a future, the gift of an education, the joy of learning, and the abiding strength of the human spirit, which is as strong and deep as the prairie grass.

Addie as a nurse

Addie lives in the Gramercy Park section of New York City.
She is currently writing about parenting and her nursing career.

Wes Jackson about Matfield Green

"… in the long run here are the people that historically have held civilization together; here are the places where the sunlight falls on the fields that provide the food and fiber that makes civilization go."

Wes Jackson is the founder and current president of The Land Institute, an organization dedicated to promoting sustainable agriculture. He is listed as one of 35 Who Made a Difference on Smithsonian.com. He received a MacArthur "genius" award in 1992 and a Right Livelihood Award in 2000.

Maps

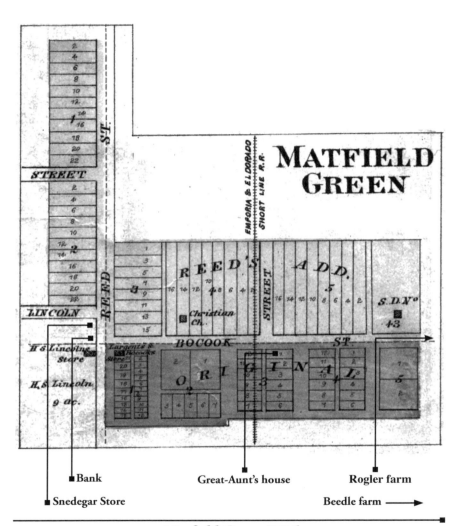

Matfield Green 1886

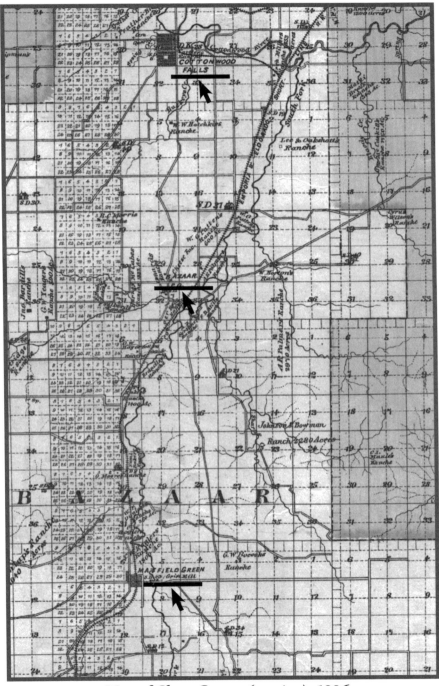

Map of Chase County (portion), 1886

Index